OREGON TRAIL STORIES

OREGON TRAIL STORIES

True Accounts of Life in a Covered Wagon

TWODOT®

GUILFORD, CONNECTICUT
HELENA, MONTANA
AN IMPRINT OF ROWMAN & LITTLEFIELD

A · TWODOT® · BOOK

TwoDot is a registered trademark of Rowman & Littlefield.

Text design by Lisa Reneson

Library of Congress Cataloging-in-Publication Data
Oregon Trail Stories: true accounts of life in a covered wagon.—1st ed.
    p. cm.
Includes bibliographical references.
ISBN-13: 978-0-7627-3082-7

    I. Oregon National Historic Trail—History—Sources. 2. Frontier and pioneer life—West (U.S.)—Sources. 3. Overland journeys to the Pacific—Sources. 4. Wagon Trains—West (U.S.)—History—Sources. 5. Pioneers—West (U.S.)—Biography. 6. Immigrants—West (U.S.)—Biography. 7. West (U.S.)—Biography. 8. West (U.S.)—History—19th century—Sources. 9. West (U.S.)—Description and travel—Sources.

F597.O75 2003
917.804'2—dc22   2003056830

Manufactured in the United States of America
Distributed by NATIONAL BOOK NETWORK

CONTENTS

"No other race of men with the means at their command would undertake so great a journey, none save these could successfully perform it, with no previous preparation, relying only on the fertility of their own invention to devise the means to overcome each danger and difficulty as it arose. They have undertaken to perform with slow-moving oxen a journey of two thousand miles. The way lies over trackless wastes, wide and deep rivers, ragged and lofty mountains and is beset with hostile savages."

Jesse Applegate, 1843

INTRODUCTION

When John Charles Frémont returned from his second expedition to the West and published *Fremont's Report of The Exploring Expedition to the Rocky Mountains in the Year 1842, and to Oregon and North California in the Years 1843-'44*, he set off a tidal wave of interest in literature about the West and turned the trickle of hardy pioneers who were braving the Great Plains for a chance at a new life in the far West into a rushing torrent. Thousands chose to travel the more than 2,000 miles to the Pacific Ocean over the Oregon Trail, writing letters, diaries, and journals as they went and memoirs of their trips years after the fact. Their stories speak of the difficulties of their decision to leave and the hardships of the trail.

The courage and fortitude of the emigrants in the largest mass migration in this country's history is perhaps what makes their stories so fascinating to us even today, but ever since the first wagon train "jumped off" from Missouri and headed west, the public has had an appetite for the tales of their adventures. Contemporary newspapers published excerpts from overland diaries, journals, and letters, inspiring many to follow in their writers' footsteps.

For some who chose the journey, the months of outdoor living and scenery unencumbered by accident, disease, or misfortune was an experience to be savored as a favorite memory for years to come. For others unexpected hardships—extremes of weather, shortages of food, water, and shelter, and the deaths of loved ones—made the trip more of a nightmare to be forgotten.

Still, "Oregon fever," drew the emigrants westward for forty years. Caravans of wagons miles wide rolled west along the network of trails, side trails, and shortcuts that made up the Oregon Trail. There were few maps and no signposts offering direction to travelers. Guides, called pilots, were hired, and natural detours caused by changes in river courses and the need for campsites with grass for livestock and fresh water were inevitable.

Among the emigrants in those caravans were men, women, and children from all over the United States; immigrants from Germany, Poland, Ireland, Russia, and other nations; and slaves and freemen of African descent. This book offers a selection of their stories, told in their own words. Today, almost all traces of the Oregon Trail have been obliterated by settlement, but these accounts of courage, stamina, and adventure survive.

SCENES AND INCIDENTS OF A PARTY OF OREGON EMIGRANTS

Lansford W. Hastings' The Emigrants Guide to Oregon and California

In 1842, twenty-three-year-old Lansford Warren Hastings, a lawyer from Mt. Vernon, Ohio, joined up with a group of emigrants heading west to the Oregon Territory at Elm Grove, Kansas, reaching the Willamette Valley in Oregon on October 5 of that year. After a brief stay in Oregon, he moved down the coast to Sutter's Fort in California, and in the summer of 1844, he returned to the East, where he published his guide-book to western emigration in 1845.

His descriptions of actual routes were of little use to the traveler, but the real purpose behind the publication was to promote Oregon and California to potential emigrants, and the book was highly successful. When the Donner Party used his guide to choose a short-cut known as the Hastings Cut-Off and met tragedy in the Sierra Nevada, the book and Hastings became widely discredited, though today it offers an intriguing glimpse of the earliest days of Oregon Trail travel.

The author long having had an anxious desire to visit those wild regions upon the great Pacific, which had now become the topic of conversation in every circle, and in reference to which, speculations both rational and irrational were everywhere in vogue, now determine to accomplish his desired object: for which purpose he repaired to Independence, Mo., which place was the known rendezvous of the Santa Fe traders, and the trappers of the Rocky mountains. Having arrived at Independence, he was so fortunate as to find, not only the Santa Fe traders, and the Rocky mountain trappers, but also a number of emigrants, consisting of families and young men who had convened there with the view of crossing the Rocky mountains, and were waiting very patiently until their number should be so increased as to afford protection and insure the safety of all, when they contemplated setting out together, for their favorite place of destination, Oregon territory. The number of emigrants continued to increase with such rapidity, that on the 15th day of May, our company consisted of one hundred and sixty persons, giving us a force of eighty armed men, which was thought ample for our protection. Having organized, and having ascertained that all had provided themselves with the necessary quantum of provisions and ammunition, as well as such teams and wagons as the company had previously determined to be essential, and indispensable, and all things else being in readiness, on the 16th day of May, in the year 1842, all as one man, united in interest, united in feeling, we were, en route, for the long desired El Dorado of the West.

Now, all was high glee, jocular hilarity, and happy anticipation, as we thus darted forward into the wild expanse, of the untrodden regions of the "western world." The harmony of feeling, the sameness of purpose, and the identity of interest, which here existed, seemed to indicate nothing but continued order, harmony and peace, amid all the trying scenes incident to our long and toilsome journey. But we had proceeded only a few days travel, from our native land of order and security, when the

"American character" was fully exhibited. All appeared to be determined to govern, but not to be governed. Here we were, without law, without order, and without restraint; in a state of nature, amid the confused, revolving fragments of elementary society! Some were sad, while others were merry; and while the brave doubted, the timid trembled! Amid this confusion, it was suggested by our captain, that we "call a halt," and pitch our tents, for the purpose of enacting, a code of laws, for the future government of the company. The suggestion was promptly complied with, when all were required to appear in their legislative capacities. When thus convened, it was urged, by the captain, as a reason why we should enact a code of laws, that an individual of the party, had proposed to capture an Indian horse, and that, he had made arrangements to accomplish his sinful purpose, by procuring a rope, and setting out with that view. In view of this alarming state of facts, it was urged by the over-legal and over-righteous, that the offending party should be immediately put upon his trial, for this enormous and wanton outrage upon Indian rights. This suggestion was also readily complied with, and the offender was soon arraigned, who, without interposing a plea to the jurisdiction, declared himself ready for trial, upon the "general issue." The investigation now commenced, during which, several speeches were delivered, abounding with severe and bitter denunciations of such highly criminal conduct, as that with which the prisoner at the bar of imaginary justice, stood charged. But it was urged on the part of the accused, that in whatever light his conduct might be viewed, by the advocates of "extreme right," it amounted to no crime at all; that to talk of taking an Indian horse, was neither malum in se, nor malum prohibitum. It was not criminal in itself, for in itself it was nothing, as he had done nothing. It was not criminal because prohibited, for in our infant state of society, we had no prohibitory code. The jury consisted of the whole company, who now with very little hesitancy, and almost unanimously, rendered their verdict of "not guilty," when the accused was discharged, and permitted to go hence, without day. Thus terminated the first jury trial, in our little community, whose government was extremely simple, yet purely democratic. This investigation, terminating as it did, afforded no valid reason for law-making, yet all being present with that view, and many being extremely anxious to accomplish the object for which they assembled, whether it was necessary or not, now proceeded to the discharge of the new, arduous and responsible duty of legislation. A committee was, therefore, appointed to draft a code of laws, for the future government of the company. This committee, contrary to the most sanguine expectations of the movers in this affair, reported that, in its opinion, no code of laws was requisite, other than the moral code, enacted by the Creator of the universe, and which is found recorded in the breast of every man. This report was adopted by an overwhelming majority, the consequence of which was, that no code of human laws was enacted; still there appeared to be a strong determination on the part of some, to do something in the way of legislating. In accordance with this determination, a decree was passed, which required the immediate and the indiscriminate extermination of the whole canine race, old and young, male and female, wherever they might be found, within our jurisdiction. This decree was passed by a very small majority, and it gave great dissatisfaction, especially to the owners of the animals whose extermination it contemplated. Those who favored its enforcement, insisted that the subjects of "the decree of death," however athletic they might be, could not possibly be taken through; that they would die before they had traveled half the distance; and that, by their incessant barking and howling, they would notify the Indians of' our locality when encamped. On the other hand, it was insisted that, if they died on the way, that would be the loss of owners, and, consequently, their business; and that if they did notify the Indians of our position, they would also notify us of theirs; and hence, the conclusion was drawn, that the advantages more than counterbalanced the disadvantages. Notwithstanding this conclusion, several dogs were slain under the inconsiderate decree, when the opposition became more general and determined. The owners of the most valuable mastiffs now declared in the most positive terms, that "if any man should kill their dogs they would kill him, regardless of all consequences." The "dog killers," however, now went out "armed and equipped," as the decree required, with a full determination to discharge their honorable and dangerous duty; but they were promptly met by the owners, who were also "armed and equipped," and prepared for any emergency. At this important crisis, the captain thought proper to convene the company again, in its legislative capacity, which being done, the "dog decree," as it was called, was almost unanimously abrogated. This was our first and last effort at legislation. This legislative rebuff, however, was not the only difficulty which we here encountered.

Our misfortunes were heightened by disease and death. The wife and child of a Mr. Lancaster were taken very ill, and the child soon died. Mrs. Lancaster remained very low for several days, during which time, the company remained in camp; but as there were no prospects of her immediate recovery, and as any considerable delay in this section, might be attended with fatal consequences to the whole company, Mr. Lancaster determined to return to the States, which he could very safely do, as we were but a few days travel from the Missouri line, and as we had passed no hostile Indians. Upon arriving at this determination, we continued our journey, and Mr. Lancaster returned to the States, where he safely arrived, as I have since learned. We passed on now very agreeably, with the exception of the occasional expression of dissatisfaction with our officers, which, however well founded, grated harshly upon the ears of the order-observing, and law-abiding portion of the company. In a very few days, we met a company of traders from Fort Larimie, on their way to the States, with their returns of furs and buffalo robes, which they had accumulated during the previous year. These furs and robes were transported in wagons, drawn by oxen. Here many of our party for the first time, saw the buffalo. The only ones, however, which they saw here, were eight or ten buffalo calves, which the traders had domesticated for the St. Louis market; and so completely domesticated were they, that they followed the cows, which had been taken out for that purpose, with very little trouble to the drivers. This meeting afforded a very favorable opportunity for forwarding letters to the States, of which many of the party were happy to avail themselves. We were informed, by this party, that we would find the buffalo upon the Platte, a few days travel below the confluence of its north and south branches: upon arriving at which place, we did find them in the greatest abundance imaginable. No adequate conception can be formed of the immensity of the numerous herds, which here abound. The entire plains and prairies are densely covered, and completely blackened with them, as far as the most acute vision extends. Now the most feverish anxiety, and confused excitement prevails. Those who are accustomed to buffalo hunting, are almost instantly upon their fleet horses, and in chase, while those unaccustomed to such scenes, "green horns," as they are called, are in the greatest confusion, adjusting saddles and martingals, tightening girths and spurs, loading guns and pistols, and giving their friends, wives and children, all manner of assurances of their unparalleled success. They too, are now ready, and like the mountaineer, they dart away, as with the wings of light; but they soon observe that they are far in the rear of the mountaineer, who is now amid the buffalo, slaying them on the right and left, in the front and rear. But stimulated by the loud thundering and clattering sounds, produced by the confused rushing forth of the thousands of frightened buffalo, as well as by the extraordinary success of the mountaineer, they ply the spur with renewed energy; and giving their fiery steeds loose rein, they are soon in the vicinity of the scene of action, but not in the scene of action, for to their utter surprise, and intolerable vexation, their heretofore faithful steeds, now decline the contest; and notwithstanding the renewed application of the spur, they merely bound, snort and plunge, but keep a respectful distance, until they arrive in the midst of the slain buffalo, which have been left by the mountaineer. Here their timidity is increased, and taking a new fright, they dart and leap away with great velocity, and notwithstanding the firm and steady restraint of the sturdy rider, they soon meet the moving caravan, to the infinite gratification of the mountaineer, the utter astonishment of the "green horn," and the sad disappointment of the friends, wives and children, who had anticipated so much from the first grand debut in buffalo hunting. The experienced hunter is soon seen returning to the camp, with his horse heavily laden with the choicest portions of some of the numerous buffalo which he has slain. In order that the company may now obtain a supply of the delicious fresh meat, with which the plains are strewed, it is directed to encamp, which having been done, all are soon abundantly supplied. Having been a few days among the buffalo, and their horses having become accustomed to these terrific scenes, even the "green horn," is enabled, not only to kill the buffalo with much expertness, but he is also frequently seen, driving them to the encampment, with as much indifference as he used formerly to drive his domestic cattle about his own fields, in the land of his nativity. Giving the buffalo rapid chase for a few minutes, they become so fatigued and completely exhausted, that they are driven from place to place, with as little difficulty as our common cattle. Both the grown buffalo and the calves, are very frequently driven in this manner to the encampment, where they are readily slaughtered.

By this time, the party had become greatly incensed with the officers, and had determined upon holding an election, for the purpose of electing other officers. Accordingly an election was held, which resulted in the election of myself to the first, and a Mr. Lovejoy to the second office of our infant republic. This election gave some dissatisfaction, to a few of the party, especially the disaffected and disappointed office-holders and office-seekers, who now, together with a few others, separated themselves from the main body, and went on a few days in advance, to Fort Larimie, where they had been but a few days, when the main body arrived. Upon arriving at Forts Larimie and John, we were received in a very kind and friendly manner by the gentlemen of those forts, who extended every attention to us, while we remained in their vicinity. While here several of our party disposed of' their oxen and wagons, taking horses in exchange. This they were induced to do, under the impression that their wagons could not be taken to Oregon, of which they were assured by the gentlemen of those forts, and other mountaineers. Many others of the party, disposed of their cows and other cattle, which had become tender footed, as from this cause, it was supposed, that they would soon, be unable to travel; but we found by experience, that by continued driving, their hoofs became more and more hardened, until they had entirely recovered. Before leaving these forts, the disaffected of our party, proposed to unite their destinies again with ours; but the main body being so exasperated with their former course, for some time refused their consent, yet in view of the fact, that they must either travel with us, remain at these forts, or return to the States, they were permitted to join us again, when, we were once more, enabled to continue our toilsome, yet interesting journey.

Leaving these forts, we had traveled but a few miles, when we met a company of trappers and traders, from Fort Hall, on their way to the States, among whom was a Mr. Fitspateric, who joined our party, as a guide, and traveled with us, as such, to Green river. From this gentleman's long residence in the great western prairies, and the Rocky mountains, he is eminently qualified as a guide, of which fact, we were fully convinced, from the many advantages which we derived from his valuable services. He was employed by Dr. White, who had received the appointment of Indian agent of Oregon, and who was under the impression, that our government would defray all such expenses; which impression, however, I think, was entirely unfounded. Perfect unanimity of feeling and purpose, now having been fully restored, we passed on very agreeably, and with little or no interruption, until we arrived at Sweet-water, near Independence rock. Here we had the misfortune to lose a young man, by the name of Bailey, who was killed by the accidental discharge of a gun. As the ball entered at the groins, and passed entirely through the body, it was readily seen, that the wound must prove fatal. He survived but about two hours, which, to him, were hours of excruciating suffering, and to us, those of gloomy despondency and grief. He was an amiable young man, a native of the state of Massachusetts; latterly from the territory of Iowa. Being a blacksmith by trade, the party sustained a great loss in his death; not only, however, in reference to his services as a mechanic, but also, in reference to the important protection, which each afforded to the other, in this wild region of savage ferocity. While he survived, every possible exertion was made to afford him relief, but all to no purpose. He constantly insisted that it was utterly impossible for him to recover, that immediate death was inevitable. The physician now gave up all hopes of his recovery; his voice faltered; death was depicted upon his countenance: and every thing seemed to indicate a speedy return of his immortal spirit, "to God who gave it," yet, even now, he was to be heard, urging us all, in the most emphatic language, to be more cautious in the future, and, thereby, avoid similar accidents. He now took his "eternal leave" of all, in the most solemn and affecting manner, at the same time, most earnestly admonishing us, "to prepare for a like fate, should it be our unhappy lot, and, at all events, to make a speedy preparation for death and eternity!" This was truly a most solemn and awful scene; and these admonitions, coming from such a source, and under such circumstances, must have produced an impressive and lasting effect! He expired in the evening, and the burial took place the next morning. The grave having been prepared, at the foot of a mountain of considerable altitude, about eighty rods southwest, from the usual encampment, we now followed to the grave, the second corpse of our little company! As we thus marched along, in solemn procession, the deepest gloom and solemnity, was depicted upon every countenance, and pungent and heartfelt grief pervaded every breast! While we were silently and solemnly moving on, under arms, "to the place of the dead," the sentinels were to be seen, standing at their designated posts, alternately meditating upon the solemnity of the passing scene, and casting their eyes watchfully around as if to descry the numerous and hostile foe, with whom we were everywhere surrounded, and thus, to avert accumulating danger! At the same time, the young man, who was the unwilling instrument of this, our trying calamity, was also to be seen, walking to and fro, suffering the most extreme mental agony; apparently noticing nothing that was transpiring around; seemingly unconscious of every thing, but his own unhappy existence, and the sad departure of his, and our lamented friend! The ordinary rites, after interment, having been performed at the grave, the company returned in the same solemn manner, to the encampment, where all sat down in silent mournful mood, contemplating the many trying scenes of the desolating past, and anticipating the dreaded fearful future!

Having spent several days at this place, and having, in the mean time, procured an additional supply of meat, re-elected our officers, and made all other necessary preparatory arrangements, we, once more, set out upon our dismal journey; when I thought proper to issue an order, which required all, in the future, to carry their guns uncapped or primed. The propriety and importance of this order, were clearly manifested, by the sad occurrence just related, hence it was readily and promptly obeyed. Had such an order been previously issued and enforced, our deceased friend might still have lived, and instead of sadness and dismay, hilarity and joy might have pervaded our community; but we, unfortunately, like thousands of others, were mere sophomores in the great school of experience. The fates, taking advantage of our want of experience, appeared really to have conspired against us; surrounding us everywhere, with the most inauspicious circumstances; and crowding our lonely way with innumerable and unforseen dangers, and with death, as if determined to deluge the whole western wilds, with human misery, and to engulf us, their defenceless victims, in the deep, dark abyss of inextricable wo; and thus, to feast upon our misfortunes, and exult triumphantly over our weakness and inexperience! Sweet-water, was a bitter water to us; if it even possessed any sweetness, it had lost it all now, for it afforded us nothing but the extreme bitterness of sore affliction and deep distress.

ACROSS THE PLAINS IN 1843

Arthur's Prairie First Furrow Plowed in Clackamas County, David Arthur, SUNDAY OREGONIAN, 1889

> *The fascination with western migration that spurred on the pioneers in the mid-nineteenth century led to an immediate public interest in their stories that has carried over to scholars and readers in more modern times. This short reminiscence is a great example of the continuing interest in those who braved the Oregon Trail.*

When in 1843 the frontier fever assumed an epidemic form on a small scale in Missouri, my parents determined to cross the desert plains to the far distant territory of Oregon. Such a journey in those days was no child's play, performed as it was with ox teams, plodding through the dust and heat, climbing mountains and swimming rivers, and not knowing one minute what the next would bring forth.

It was men of the character and disposition to face such dangers accompanied by their heroic wives, mothers and sisters, who severed all connecting them with home and civilization and struck out boldly upon a trackless desert, known to be inhabited by howling wolves and merciless savages, surrounded by dangers, seen and unseen, who I undertake to say, were the chief event to save Oregon to the United States. Hence, I was a pioneer from necessity and in fact, and have ever looked at it without romantic coloring, but as a stern reality to fulfill a duty or destiny.

The early pioneers were forced to live mosly on bread and boiled wheat and drink pea coffee. They lived in log cabins, slept on blankets wore moccasins and buckskin pants, and endured many trials and difficulties.

I drove the foremost team down from the summit of the Blue Mountains that ever made a track on Umatilla soil and plowed the first 40 acres of land, if not the first furrow ever plowed in Clackamas County, the winter of 43, seven miles East of Oregon City, for my father, in what has been called the "Arthur Prairie" ever since that date, and lived in Oregon three long and doubtful years before the question of title to Oregon was settled between Great Britain and the United States, June 15, 1846.

I have lived under the provisional government, then the territorial government and have remained in the Willamette valley ever since Oregon was admitted into the sisterhood of states. I hold that I fulfilled my allotted part in the development of the natural resources of the country: but my labor has passed into the hands of others.

The lonely hut of the savage is gone and in its place are stately temples; the ravenous beast has fled from the face of man, and the valleys are all golden with ripening grain that awaits the harvester.

The beautiful Willamette runs onward to the Columbia as it did in the days of yore; the broad Columbia rolls its everlasting tide into the Pacific as it did when Bryant sang its praises to the world, but the light canoe is replaced by the mammoth steamship, and the shriek of the locomotive hourly wakes the sleeping echoes of its pine-fringed shores.

FROM THE LETTERS OF
NARCISSA WHITMAN

Narcissa Prentiss and Marcus Whitman were married on February 18, 1836, and the next day they began the journey that took them west to Waiilatpu in the Oregon Country, near what is now the town of Walla-Walla, Washington, where they were to be missionaries to the local Native American tribes.

Narcissa was one of the first two white women to cross the continent overland, and she had the first child born of American parents in the Oregon Country. Once settled there, she began an extensive correspondence about her life with her family in the East that lasted until her death on November 29, 1847, when she, her husband, and eleven emigrants at the mission were attacked and murdered by a renegade band of local Native Americans.

Hon. Stephen Prentiss
Cuba, Allegheny Co., New York.
WAIILATPU
Oct. 9th, 1844.

Beloved and Honored Parents:

I have no unanswered letters on hand, either from dear father and mother or any of the family, yet I cannot refrain from writing every stated opportunity. The season has arrived when the emigrants are beginning to pass us on their way to the Willamette. Last season there were such a multitude of starving people passed us that quite drained us of all our provisions, except potatoes. Husband has been endeavoring this summer to cultivate so as to be able to impart without so much distressing ourselves. In addition to this, he has been obliged to build a mill, and to do it principally with his own hands, which has rendered it exceedingly laborious for him. In the meantime, I have endeavored to lighten his burden as much as possible in superintending the ingathering of the garden, etc. During this period, the Indians belonging to this station and the Nez Perces go to Forts Hall and Boise to meet the emigrants for the purpose of trading their wornout cattle for horses. Last week Tuesday, several young men arrived, the first of the party that brought us any definite intelligence concerning them (having nothing but Indian reports previous), among whom was a youth from Rushville formerly, of the name of Gilbert, one of husband's scholars.

Last Friday a family of eight arrived, including the grandmother, an aged woman, probably as old, or older than my mother. Several such persons have passed, both men and women, and I often think when I gaze upon them, shall I ever be permitted to look upon the face of my dear parents in this land?

25th-When I commenced this letter I intended to write a little every day, so as to give you a picture of our situation at this time. But it has been impossible. Now I must write as briefly as possible and send off my letter, or lose the opportunity. The emigration is late in getting into the country. It is now the last of October and they have just begun to arrive with their wagons. The Blue mountains are covered with snow, and many families, if not half of the party, are back in or beyond the mountains, and what is still worse, destitute or provisions and some of them of clothing. Many are sick, several with children born on the way. One family arrived here night before last, and the next morn a child was born; another is expected in the same condition.

Here we are, one family alone, a way mark, as it were, or center post, about which multitudes will or must gather this winter. And these we must feed and warm to the extent of our powers. Blessed by God that He has given us so abundantly of the fruit of the earth that we may impart to those who are thus famishing. Two preachers with large families are here and wish to stay for the winter, both Methodist. With all this upon our hands, besides our duties and labors for the Indians, can any one think we lack employment or have any time to be idle?

Mr. and Mrs. Littlejohn left us in September and have gone below to settle in the Willamette. We have been looking for associated this fall, but the Board could get none ready, but say, they will send next year. Am I ever to see any of my family among the tide of emigration that is flowing west?

Our mill is finished and grinds well. It is a mill out of doors or without a house; that we must build next year.

We have employed a young man of the party to teach school, so that we hope to have both an English school and one for the natives. My health has been improving remarkably through the summer, and one great means has been daily bathing in the river. I was very miserable one year ago now, and was brought very low and poor; now I am better than I have been for some time, and quite fleshly for me. I weigh one hundred and sixty-seven pounds; much higher than ever before in my life. This will make the girls laugh, I know. Mrs. Spaulding's health is better than last year. She expects an increase in her family soon.

This country is destined to be filled, and we desire greatly to have good people come, and ministers and Christians, that it may be saved from being a sink of wickedness and prostitution. We need many houses to accommodate the families that will be obliged to winter here. All the house room that we have to spare is filled already. It is expected that there are more than five hundred souls back in the snow and mountains. Among the number is an orphan family of seven children, the youngest an infant born on the way, whose parents have both died since they left the States. Application has been made for us to take them, as they have not a relative in the company. What we shall do I cannot say; we cannot see them suffer, if the Lord casts them upon us. He will give us His grace and strength to do our duty to them.

I cannot write any more, I am so thronged and employed that I feel sometimes like being crazy, and my poor husband, if he had a hundred strings tied to him pulling in every direction, could not be any worse off.

Dear parents, do pray earnestly for your children here, for their situation is one of great trial, as well as of responsibility.

Love from us both to you all. I am disappointed in not getting letters from some of the dear ones this fall, but so it must be and I submit.

Your affectionate daughter
NARCISSA

ON THE PLAINS IN 1844

Catherine Sager Pringle, Across the Plains in 1844
ca. 1860

> *Catherine Sager Pringle's account of her cross-country trip
> with her family in 1844 was written as a memoir approx-
> imately sixteen years after the events recounted here.
> Orphaned by illness on the arduous journey west, she and her
> six brothers and sisters were taken in by Marcus and
> Narcissa Whitman at their mission near present-day Walla-
> Walla, Washington. Thirteen-year-old Catherine would sur-
> vive the massacre of the Whitmans, two of her brothers, and
> other emigrants in 1847.*

My father was one of the restless ones who are not content to remain in
one place long at a time. Late in the fall of 1838 we emigrated from Ohio
to Missouri. Our first halting place was on Green River, but the next year
we took a farm in Platte County. He engaged in farming and black-
smithing, and had a wide reputation for ingenuity. Anything they needed,
made or mended, sought his shop. In 1843, Dr. Whitman came to
Missouri. The healthful climate induced my mother to favor moving to
Oregon. Immigration was the theme all winter, and we decided to start
for Oregon. Late in 1843 father sold his property and moved near St.
Joseph, and in April, 1844, we started across the plains. The first

encampments were a great pleasure to us children. We were five girls and two boys, ranging from the girl baby to be born on the way to the oldest boy, hardly old enough to be any help.

Starting on the Plains

We waited several days at the Missouri River. Many friends came that far to see the emigrants start on their long journey, and there was much sadness at the parting, and a sorrowful company crossed the Missouri that bright spring morning. The motion of the wagon made us all sick, and it was weeks before we got used to the seasick motion. Rain came down and required us to tie down the wagon covers, and so increased our sickness by confining the air we breathed.

Our cattle recrossed in the night and went back to their winter quarters. This caused delay in recovering them and a weary, forced march to rejoin the train. This was divided into companies, and we were in that commanded by William Shaw. Soon after starting Indians raided our camp one night and drove off a number of cattle. They were pursued, but never recovered.

Soon everything went smooth and our train made steady headway. The weather was fine and we enjoyed the journey pleasantly. There were several musical instruments among the emigrants, and these sounded clearly on the evening air when camp was made and merry talk and laughter resounded from almost every camp-fire.

Incidents of Travel

We had one wagon, two steady yoke of old cattle, and several of young and not well-broken ones. Father was no ox driver, and had trouble with these until one day he called on Captain Shaw for assistance. It was furnished by the good captain pelting the refractory steers with stones until they were glad to come to terms.

Reaching the buffalo country, our father would get some one to drive his team and start on the hunt, for he was enthusiastic in his love of such sport. He not only killed the great bison, but often brought home on his shoulder the timid antelope that had fallen at his unerring aim, and that are not often shot by ordinary marksmen. Soon after crossing South Platte the unwieldy oxen ran on a bank and overturned the wagon, greatly injuring our mother. She lay long insensible in the tent put up for the occasion.

August 1st we nooned in a beautiful grove on the north side of the Platte. We had by this time got used to climbing in and out of the wagon when in motion. When performing this feat that afternoon my dress caught on an axle helve and I was thrown under the wagon wheel, which passed over and badly crushed my limb before father could stop the team. He picked me up and saw the extent of the injury when the injured limb hung dangling in the air.

The Father Dying on the Plains

In a broken voice he exclaimed: "My dear child, your leg is broken all to pieces!" The news soon spread along the train and a halt was called. A surgeon was found and the limb set; then we pushed on the same night to Laramie, where we arrived soon after dark. This accident confined me to the wagon the remainder of the long journey.

After Laramie we entered the great American desert, which was hard on the teams. Sickness became common. Father and the boys were all sick, and we were dependent for a driver on the Dutch doctor who set my leg. He offered his services and was employed, but though an excellent surgeon, he knew little about driving oxen. Some of them often had to rise from their sick beds to wade streams and get the oxen safely across. One day four buffalo ran between our wagon and the one behind. Though feeble, father seized his gun and gave chase to them. This imprudent act prostrated him again, and it soon became apparent that his days were numbered. He was fully conscious of the fact, but could not be reconciled to the thought of leaving his large and helpless family in such precarious circumstances. The evening before his death we crossed Green River and camped on the bank. Looking where I lay helpless, he said: "Poor child! What will become of you?" Captain Shaw found him weeping bitterly. He said his last hour had come, and his heart was filled with anguish for his family. His wife was ill, the children small, and one likely to be a cripple. They had no relatives near, and a long journey lay before them. In piteous tones he begged the Captain to take charge of them and see them through. This he stoutly promised. Father was buried the next day on the banks of Green River. His coffin was made of two troughs dug out of the body of a tree, but next year emigrants found his bleaching bones, as the Indians had disinterred the remains.

We hired a young man to drive, as mother was afraid to trust the doctor, but the kindhearted German would not leave her, and declared his intention to see her safe in the Willamette. At Fort Bridger the stream was full of fish, and we made nets of wagon sheets to catch them. That evening the new driver told mother he would hunt for game if she would let him use the gun. He took it, and we never saw him again. He made for the train in advance, where he had a sweetheart. We found the gun waiting our arrival at Whitman's. Then we got along as best we could with the doctor's help.

Mother planned to get to Whitman's and winter there, but she was rapidly failing under her sorrows. The nights and mornings were very cold, and she took cold from the exposure unavoidably. With camp fever and a sore mouth, she fought bravely against fate for the sake of her children, but she was taken delirious soon after reaching Fort Bridger, and was bed-fast. Travelling in this condition over a road clouded with dust, she suffered intensely. She talked of her husband, addressing him as though present, beseeching him in piteous tones to relieve her sufferings, until at last she became unconscious. Her babe was cared for by the women of the train. Those kind-hearted women would also come in at night and wash the dust from the mother's face and otherwise make her comfortable. We travelled a rough road the day she died, and she moaned fearfully all the time. At night one of the women came in as usual, but she made no reply to questions, so she thought her asleep, and washed her face, then took her hand and discovered the pulse was nearly gone. She lived but a few moments, and her last words were, "Oh, Henry! If you only knew how we have suffered." The tent was set up, the corpse laid out, and next morning we took the last look at our mother's face. The grave was near the road; willow brush was laid in the bottom and covered the body, the earth filled in—then the train moved on.

Her name was cut on a headboard, and that was all that could be done. So in twenty-six days we became orphans. Seven children of us, the oldest fourteen and the youngest a babe. A few days before her death, finding herself in possession of her faculties and fully aware of the coming end, she had taken an affectionate farewell of her children and charged the doctor to take care of us. She made the same request of Captain Shaw. The baby was taken by a woman in the train, and all were literally adopted by the company. No one there but was ready to do us any possible favor. This was especially true of Captain Shaw and his wife. Their kindness will ever be cherished in grateful remembrance by us all. Our parents could not have been more solicitous or careful. When our flour gave out they gave us bread as long as they had any, actually dividing their last loaf. To this day Uncle Billy and Aunt Sally, as we call them, regard us with the affection of parents. Blessings on his hoary head!

At Snake River they lay by to make our wagon into a cart, as our team was wearing out. Into this was loaded what was necessary. Some things were sold and some left on the plains. The last of September we arrived at

Grande Ronde, where one of my sister's clothes caught fire, and she would have burned to death only that the German doctor, at the cost of burning his hands, saved her. One night the captain heard a child crying, and found my little sister had got out of the wagon and was perishing in the freezing air, for the nights were very cold. We had been out of flour and living on meat alone, so a few were sent in advance to get supplies from Dr. Whitman and return to us. Having so light a load we could travel faster than the other teams, and went on with Captain Shaw and the advance. Through the Blue Mountains cattle were giving out and left lying in the road. We made but a few miles a day. We were in the country of "Dr. Whitman's Indians," as they called themselves. They were returning from buffalo hunting and frequented our camps. They were loud in praise of the missionaries and anxious to assist us. Often they would drive up some beast that had been left behind as given out and return it to its owner.

One day when we were making a fire of wet wood Francis thought to help the matter by holding his powder-horn over a small blaze. Of course the powder-horn exploded, and the wonder was he was left alive. He ran to a creek near by and bathed his hands and face, and came back destitute of winkers and eyebrows, and his face was blackened beyond recognition. Such were the incidents and dangerous and humorous features of the journey.

We reached Umatilla October 15th, and lay by while Captain Shaw went on to Whitman's station to see if the doctor would take care of us, if only until he could become located in the Willamette. We purchased of the Indians the first potatoes we had eaten since we started on our long and sad journey. October 17th we started for our destination, leaving the baby very sick, with doubts of its recovery. Mrs. Shaw took an affectionate leave of us all, and stood looking after us as long as we were in sight. Speaking of it in later years, she said she never saw a more pitiful sight than that cartful of orphans going to find a home among strangers.

We reached the station in the forenoon. For weeks this place had been a subject for our talk by day and formed our dreams at night. We expected to see log houses, occupied by Indians and such people as we had seen about the forts. Instead we saw a large white house surrounded with palisades. A short distance from the doctor's dwelling was another large adobe house, built by Mr. Gray, but now used by immigrants in the winter, and for a granary in the summer. It was situated near the mill pond, and the grist mill was not far from it.

Between the two houses were the blacksmith shop and the corral, enclosed with slabs set up endways. The garden lay between the mill and the house, and a large field was on the opposite side. A good-sized ditch passed in front of the house, connecting with the mill pond, intersecting other ditches all around the farm, for the purpose of irrigating the land.

We drove up and halted near this ditch. Captain Shaw was in the house conversing with Mrs. Whitman. Glancing through the window, he saw us, and turning to her said: "Your children have come; will you go out and see them?" He then came out and told the boys to "Help the girls out and get their bonnets." Alas! it was easy to talk of bonnets, but not to find them! But one or two were finally discovered by the time Mrs. Whitman had come out. Here was a scene for an artist to describe! Foremost stood the little cart, with the tired oxen that had been unyoked lying near it. Sitting in the front end of the cart was John, weeping bitterly; on the opposite side stood Francis, his arms on the wheel and his head resting on his arms, sobbing aloud; on the near side the little girls were huddled together, bareheaded and barefooted, looking at the boys and then at the house, dreading we knew not what. By the oxen stood the good German doctor, with his whip in his hand, regarding the scene with suppressed emotion.

Thus Mrs. Whitman found us. She was a large, well-formed woman, fair complexioned, with beautiful auburn hair, nose rather large, and large gray eyes. She had on a dark calico dress and gingham sunbonnet. We thought as we shyly looked at her that she was the prettiest woman we had ever seen. She spoke kindly to us as she came up, but like frightened things we ran behind the cart, peeping shyly around at her. She then addressed the boys, asking why they wept, adding: "Poor boys. no wonder you weep!" She then began to arrange things as we threw them out, at the same time conversing with an Indian woman sitting on the ground near by.

A little girl about seven years old soon came and stood regarding us with a timid look. This was little Helen Mar Meed, and though a half-breed, she looked very pretty to us in her green dress and white apron and neat sunbonnet.

Having arranged everything in compact form Mrs. Whitman directed the doctor and the boys where to carry them, and told Helen to show the little girls the way to the house. Seeing my lameness, she kindly took me by the hand and my little sister by the other hand, and thus led us in. As we reached the steps, Captain Shaw asked if she had children of her own. Pointing to a grave at the foot of the hill not far off, she said: "All the child I ever had sleeps yonder." She added that it was a great pleasure to her that she could see the grave from the door. The doctor and boys having deposited the things as directed, went over to the mansion. As we entered the house we saw a girl about nine years old washing dishes. Mrs. Whitman spoke cheerfully to her and said: "Well, Mary Ann, how do you think you will like all these sisters?" Seated in her arm-chair, she placed the youngest on her lap, and calling us round her, asked our names, about our parents, and the baby, often exclaiming as we told our artless story, "Poor children!"

Dr. Whitman came in from the mill and stood in the door, looking as though surprised at the large addition so suddenly made to the family. We were a sight calculated to excite surprise, dirty and sunburned until we looked more like Indians than white children. Added to this, John had cropped our hair so that it hung in uneven locks and added to our uncouth appearance. Seeing her husband standing there, Mrs. Whitman said, with a laugh: "Come in, doctor, and see your children." He sat down and tried to take little Louisa in his arms, but she ran screaming to me, much to the discomfiture of the doctor and amusement of his wife. She then related to him what we had told her in reference to the baby, and expressed her fears lest it should die, saying it was the baby she wanted most of all.

Our mother had asked that we might not be separated, so Captain Shaw now urged the doctor to take charge of us all. He feared the Board might object, as he was sent a missionary to the Indians. The captain argued that a missionary's duty was to do good, and we certainly were objects worthy of missionary charity. He was finally persuaded to keep us all until spring. His wife did not readily consent, but he told her he wanted boys as well as she girls. Finding the boys willing to stay, he made a written agreement with Captain Shaw that he would take charge of them. Before Captain Show reached the valley, Dr. Whitman overtook him and told him he was pleased with the children and he need give himself no further care concerning them. The baby was brought over in few days. It was very sick, but under Mrs. Whitman's judicious care was soon restored to health.

Our faithful friend, the German doctor, left us at last, safe in the motherly care of Mrs. Whitman. Well had he kept his promise to our dying mother.

For a week or two the house at Waiilatpu was full of company. Having no help, Mrs. Whitman was too much engaged in household affairs to pay any attention to us. Very lonely did that large house seem to me during that time. Being a cripple, I was not able to join the other children in their pastimes, and they were too busy enjoying themselves to attend to me. Seated by the cradle, I plied my needle at simple sewing. I saw my brothers only at meal-time. Mrs. Whitman came occasionally to bring the baby her milk.

I thought I could never be happy where everything was so strange, and shed many tears in solitude. I became so timid as to cry if addressed by the doctor or any one.

School commenced soon after our arrival, and most of the children attended. In course of time the company left the home; help was hired to do the housework, and Mrs. Whitman, having more time to herself, paid more to us. Gathering us around her in the evening, she amused us with anecdotes, distributing pieces of calico and showing us how to make patchwork and rag dolls, conversing with us in a kind and familiar way. On one of these occasions she gave each of us a string of beads to wear, with the understanding that any one who had to be reproved for doing wrong must return the beads to her. We had been long without restraint, so that we had become quite unruly and difficult to manage. They were strict disciplinarians, and held the reins with steady hands. Any deviation from the rules met with instant and severe chastisement. Every effort to merit their approval was rewarded with smiles. While we were held under strict subjection, every effort was made to render us comfortable and happy and to win our love and confidence. Mrs. Whitman was particularly adapted to raising children, having the art of uniting instruction and pleasure. She was a fine singer. I have never known any one who excelled her in this respect. She soon commenced teaching us vocal music. Refined and accomplished herself, she exercised over our rude natures that influence that refines and beautifies a home. We soon formed a warm attachment for her, and fell into the practice of calling her and Dr. Whitman mother and father, as the other children did, and continued it while they lived. They were careful to have us remember our parents, and would speak of them with affection and respect. When necessary to administer punishment, she would set our fault before us and her own responsibility, and show that all was done for our own good, and would ask what we thought our parents would wish her to do.

Dr. Whitman's family, before we came, consisted of himself and wife, Perrin P. Whitman, his nephew, who came out with him in 1843, when fourteen years old; Mary Ann Bridger, nine years old; Helen Mar Meek, seven years old, who had been raised from infancy by Mrs. Whitman, and David M. Cortez, seven years old. This boy's father was a Spaniard, his mother a Walla Walla Indian. Becoming tired of the infant, she cast it into a hole to perish. His grandmother rescued him and took him to Mrs. Whitman, naked, except a small piece of skin tied over his shoulders. We were in the schoolroom from Monday morning until Saturday noon. The afternoon was a holiday. If the weather was pleasant, the preparations for the Sabbath being completed, Mrs. Whitman took us out for a ramble over the hills. In inclement weather we were provided amusement in the house; the doctor believed in young folks having plenty of exercise. The Sabbath was always strictly observed, yet made so pleasant that we hailed its dawn with delight. Every preparation was made the day before, and perfect stillness pervaded the house Sabbath morning. In the winter season a Bible class met on Saturday night. All the family attended, and no effort was spared to make it interesting. A subject was given us to prove from the Bible, and Mrs. Whitman saw that each child had a proof to bring in. They were commented on, a chapter was read, each one reading a verse and giving their thoughts on it. These exercises closed by singing some Bible hymn. Sabbath morning we were reminded of the day and all kept still. Each sat with a book, and those too small to read were handed pictures. After breakfast we prepared for Sunday school, that met at 11 o'clock, while the doctor held his service with the natives. Each got seven verses, one being learned every morning during the week. This was an interesting hour spent together, especially when the doctor could spend some moments with us. At 3 P.M. we met for the regular afternoon service, when Dr. Whitman read a sermon. He was not a preacher, but a physician. We had to find the text after the service was over and repeat it to him.

The evening was spent in reading, reciting the commandments, etc.

One evening in the week Mrs. Whitman would collect the young around her, holding a prayer meeting with them and conversing on religious subjects. The first Monday night in each month a meeting was held in behalf of missions, and Monday after New Year's was observed as a fast day. The housework was hired done in winter, so the children could follow their studies without hindrance; Mrs. Whitman and the girls did the work in the summer. Each of us had her alloted task and was expected to promptly do her duty. At 11 we bathed in the river; dinner was served at 12. When the work was done we all sat in a large room at our sewing, save one of us, who read aloud to the rest. Supper was at 5 o'clock, and after that was over time until retiring for the night was devoted to recreation. In the spring the evenings were spent in the garden putting in seeds; otherwise we did as we pleased. Sometimes the boys would bring horses for us to ride; at times we would go with the doctor to visit the lodges, where Indians were sick. Mrs. Whitman was always with us in all these occupations, adding to our enjoyment. She was very fond of flowers, and we assisted in taking care of her flower garden each season. Our time flowed on in one uninterrupted stream of pleasure; we were kept constantly gaining knowledge, and from morning until night our adopted parents labored to promote our happiness. The family was larger in the winter. From twenty to twenty-five, including children, sat around the table at meals. Besides the adopted children, there were others who came to attend the mission school. Summers the doctor was gone most of the time, so there was only Mrs. Whitman and the children. Mr. Spaulding's daughter attended school with us. She came on horseback, in charge of an Indian woman, 120 miles.

The manner of living was simple. In winter we had beef, and in summer mutton and fish. Pork seldom came on the table. Dr. Whitman ignored fine flour, and wheat flour and corn meal were used unbolted. Tea and coffee came to the table only on rare occasions. This was a matter of economy as delicacies were not easy to get in the country at that time. There was an abundance of wild fruit to be purchased of the natives; a good garden supplied plenty of vegetables. Cake and pastry only were seen on holidays. Milk, butter and cheese were in full supply, and thus you have our mode of living at Waiilatpu.

Some may ask how the washing for so large a family was managed. As early as 4 o'clock all hands were mustered for work in the kitchen, Mrs. Whitman at the head. Tubs and barrels were put in use, and all the implements needed were at hand. The boys, with long aprons tied around them, brought the water and did the pounding, while the women rubbed the clothes. Jokes were current and all were in good humor. By school time (9 o'clock) the clothes were on the line. It fell to the lot of myself and brother to get breakfast on wash days.

Owing to the location and the evaporation in the spring of alkali ponds near by, Waiilatpu was not healthy. The mill pond was near by, and we were more or less troubled with chills and fever in warm weather. I was very subject to it, and suffered every summer of my stay there, being often unable to labor. As the eldest daughter, I had supervision of the other girls, and from being confined to the house so much I became the constant companion of Mrs. Whitman. An attachment near to that of mother and daughter existed between us from this constant association. To me she told all her plans for the pleasure or improvement of the children, as well as her fears and troubles concerning them. When the doctor was long absent I sat with her and read or conversed, and was her bedfellow. She said often she could not get along without me.

The spring after we arrived brother Francis resolved to run away to the lower country with those who had wintered there. His reason was he disliked the strict discipline maintained. The doctor was away, and when Francis started to go Mrs. Whitman urged him pleasantly to stay, but he went on the run, mounted his horse, and was off before the wagons moved which he was to accompany. She had not succeeded in winning the boy's confidence and affection, and Francis was stubborn.

Efforts were made to overtake him and get him to come back, but they were unavailing. He went to the Willamette and remained there.

On his return Dr. Whitman talked with John and found he was willing to remain. He then made a proposal to aid the boys to get a start in cattle and horses, so that they would be acquiring property. This was made known to Francis by a letter, and a horse sent for him, so that in the fall we had the pleasure of again becoming a united family.

In the spring of 1845 the Cayuses were embroiled in war with the Snakes. A Cayuse family named Prince was going to the buffalo country to hunt, and on the way camped on a small stream in the Snake region, opposite a camp of Snake Indians. One morning Prince with his servant rode over to see the other camp. His horse stood all day tied at the Snake lodge, but the mother did not go to learn about him, because her daughter said it would be foolish. Toward night the horse disappeared, and during the night the Snake camp also disappeared. Going over there, the mother and daughter found the dead bodies of servant and master. War resulted, in which many Cayuses lost their lives, including some of their chiefs. We saw them come home from their war raids, and heard and saw them singing war songs, dancing their war dances, and then they would change to a funeral dirge for their dead warriors. After a successful raid they would spend days in celebrating their victory and reciting the prowess of their own warriors. The beating of drums and their war-whoops and songs filled the air with savage sounds. The monotonous tones of the Indian flute mellowed the horrors of the din a little.

One Sunday morning in the autumn of 1845 two men arrived at the station. One of them, Andrew Rodgers, was a young man of about twenty-five, tall and slender, sandy hair and sallow look that betokened ill-health. He sang hymns and played the violin, so the "Seceders," to which church he belonged, turned him out. His gentlemanly appearance and intelligence won the admiration of Dr. and Mrs. Whitman. He came to procure room and care for a friend who was ill with consumption. He succeeded in this and was also engaged to teach school the ensuing winter. Going to Umatilla, he soon returned with his friend, Joseph Finly, who took board with the family of Mr. Osborne, his relative. He had made the journey to Oregon hoping for improved health. For awhile he improved and seemed stronger. Dr. and Mrs. Whitman became much attached to him. He was one day taken worse when at their house and never left it. They made him comfortable and attended to him as if he were a son or brother. He died very happy, bidding all good-by and thanking his friends for all their care of him. All gathered round the death-bed, and the scene was very impressive as he gave his last farewell to all around him.

About this time the station had a visit from a band of Delaware Indians, under the leadership of Tom Hill, who was very intelligent and could speak English as well as Cayuse. Dr. Whitman made a feast for them and invited the leading Cayuses and others. The indispensable item of an Indian feast was corn mush. A large kettle was suspended over a fire in the yard and the mush was made by putting in tallow and stirring in meal or flour. When cooked the kettle was taken indoors and placed on the floor. The doctor was master of ceremonies and the rest came in order of rank. The doctor and the chiefs dipped their spoons in the big kettle, but common people had dishes served and ate out of them. Some acted as waiters. They had tea, sweetened. We children were looking on, and it amused us to see what a quantity of sugar they used—all that the tea could hold. It was evening and the family occupied a bench on one side of the big room, which was crowded. It was well lighted with candles, and they ate in silence, except the sipping noise peculiar to Indians eating. Their performances at the trencher were so amusing to us that occasionally Mrs. Whitman had to send us outdoors to have our laugh out. When the feast was over the room was cleared and put in order for the speech. Tom Hill delivered an address that lasted two hours and was quite eloquent. We could understand the Cayuse talk, but the Indians did not know it. We were not allowed to learn it, and kept as much as possible away from the Indians, but constantly hearing the language spoken, we could not help but learn the meaning of it, though we could not speak it well. After the massacre they soon found out that we understood their talk. Mrs. Whitman always treated them politely and kindly, thanking them for every little favor they did her.

The next spring Mr. Rogers was away much of the time at the Spokane mission, conducted by Messrs. Walker and Eells. Dr. Whitman was absent at the saw mill or breaking up land for the Indians and plotting in their crops. Mrs. Whitman and the girls spent the time at home and found enough to employ them to prevent feeling lonesome. We studied botany with her and rambled over the country in search of flowers and plants.

A bad man was named Tam-a-has, meaning murderer, as he had once killed a man. One day the doctor was at work in his field when this man rode up and ordered him, peremptorily, to go and grind a grist for him. When the doctor objected to his talking and acting so, he said he could grind it for himself, and started for the mill. The doctor could walk across sooner and did so. Tam-a-has came at him there with a club, but saw an iron bar in his hand. They had a serious time of it, both with words and blows, but the iron bar was a full match for the club, and Tam-a-has finally agreed to behave himself and have his grist ground. Exhausted in body and mind, the doctor came to the house and threw himself down, saying that if they would only say so he would gladly leave, for he was tired almost beyond endurance.

It is hardly possible to conceive of a greater change than Dr. Whitman had worked in the life of the Cayuses. They had now growing fields, could have good homes, a mill to grind their meal, and they were taught things of the greatest use, yet some of them could not realize that he was unselfish in all this.

The following winter was very cold, the coldest ever known in the country and the Indians charged the whites with bringing the cold weather upon them. Old Jimmy, a Catholic Indian, claimed the power of working miracles, and said he brought the cold upon them to punish them for their unbelief and wickedness. They paid him liberally to bring about a change, and finally a thaw did come and he claimed all the merit of it.

The doctor made his fall visit to the valley, bringing back something for each one of us. He always remembered the children when he went to the valley, and brought us all some token of his love. He piloted the emigrants by a nearer and better route to The Dalles, and learned with apprehension that the last of the train were afflicted with measles and whooping cough. He knew they would spread through the native camps and feared the consequences. None of his own family had had the measles and but few of the others.

This fall brother John had his horse saddled to return to The Dalles to reside, but at Mr. Whitman's earnest request he consented to remain. Had he gone there he might now be living! Laying aside his gun, he now devoted himself to his studies. He rose early, at 4 o'clock, and wrote, but I never knew what he wrote about, as the papers were all destroyed after the massacre.

The measles were among the natives, and in the doctor's absence Mrs. Whitman was their physician. All arrangements were made for the winter, teachers were employed, and all things were in order. The emigration had brought a Canadian half-breed named Jo Lewis, who was so disagreeable that they refused to let him travel farther in their company. Dr. Whitman reluctantly gave him some work. He tried to send him below with a company, but in a few days he was back again, so the doctor reluctantly engaged him for the winter. He was destitute of clothes and was supplied. We all disliked him, but he was well used and kindly treated. Yet this wretch laid the careful plans and told the terrible lies that led to the massacre, and took an active part in murder and robbery.

REMINISCENCES OF A TRIP ACROSS THE PLAINS IN '45

Lucy Jane Hall Burnett

> *One of the many memoirs of overland emigration written long after the fact, Lucy Jane Hall Burnett's account of the wagon train she was a part of as a child gives a glimpse of one of the more infamous incidents of the great migration. Stephen H. L. Meek was anxious to gain a reputation as a pilot on the Oregon Trail and as a result of his ambition led a wagon train, which became known as "The Lost Meeks," wandering through a parched desert on an untried short cut that actually added many weeks to the crossing.*

My father, Lawrence Hall, was elected captain of our train, and we started on our way with thirty wagons and about fifty men.

A wedding occurred in our company. The bride's cake was made with turtle eggs found in the creek. The event was celebrated by a dance on the grass under the stars.

Near Ft. Boise the Indians made an attempt to attack our train and stampede the stock, but failed through the prompt action of my father, who ordered the teams unhitched and the wagons formed in a circle with the tongues of each run under the wagon just forward, making a strong barricade. The oxen were put inside, each driver standing by his own team. The women and children were also inside by the wagons. All the available men were outside standing with guns drawn. The captain walked out alone toward the Indians with his gun in one hand and a white flag in the other. He motioned the Indians not to come any nearer or his men would fire upon them. The Indians turned and ran away as fast as their horses could go. They had fine horses. The men were nude and painted.

Our most serious troubles began when we took the Stephen Meek cut-off. He represented that this route was much shorter than the other, and that there was no danger from the Indians, as this way did not lead through the Snake River Indians' territory. By vote it was decided to follow Mr. Meek. A contract was signed to pay him for his services, and he agreed to pilot the company safely through in thirty days, or, as was written in his own words, give his head for a football. All were to take turns hauling his goods. He and his wife were on horseback.

One day, after three weeks' travel on our new route, our guide suddenly and excitedly exclaimed, "My God, we are lost." Alarmed, but not dismayed, we moved on till night. There was neither grass nor water to be found. All night the men sat by the dim camp fires listening for reports from those who had gone in search of water. If any was found a signal of three shots was to be fired in quick succession; if not three shots at intervals. At sunrise no sound had been heard. The train was soon moving on through sage brush and across dry creek beds which mocked our thirst. So we journeyed till noon, when hark! a shot, but not the three in quick succession, but at intervals; like a death knell they sounded. The men stood in groups talking over the situation, the mothers, pale and haggard, sat in the wagons with their little ones around them. With a determination that knows not defeat the party moved on. About night in quick succession shots were heard, which proclaimed that water had been found. All pushed forward with renewed energy. When in sight of the water the thirsty oxen broke into a run and rushed into the water and drank until they had to be driven out.

"We are saved, we are saved! Thank God!" cried Stephen Meek, "for now I know the way." He could locate the trail to The Dalles from this stream. Men, women and children were laughing and crying in turn.

The teams were in such a bad condition that we had to lay by here three weeks. Many were sick and some died and were laid to rest in this camp. Mr. Meek would certainly have given his head for a football, had not he and his wife made their timely escape. When we reached the Deschutes the Indians there made us understand that a man and woman had crossed the river a short time before. The man swam the river, leading his horse, and an Indian swam over with the woman on his back. Other Indians tied her clothes on their heads and swam across. We did not hear of the Meeks for more than a year after this.

We were lost in the mountains six weeks. The way was rough beyond description. The women and children walked most of the way.

On reaching The Dalles Meek told the missionaries there that a party of emigrants were in the mountains. A white man and two Indians were at once sent in search of our company. When found we people were on the verge of starvation. But for the provisions brought by the scouts many, if not all, would have perished, as it took a week more to reach The Dalles when guided by these men.

CROSSING THE PLAINS IN 1846

As told by Mrs. Mary Elizabeth Munkers Estes, 1916

> *In her eighties when she told this tale of her family's journey over the Oregon Trail and settlement in what is now Oregon, Mary Elizabeth Munkers Estes offered reminiscences that are a valuable piece of Oregon history.*

From nearby Liberty, Missouri, in early April 1846, about fifty families prepared to make the journey to the far away Oregon Territory, which then included what is now the states of Oregon, Washington, Idaho and part of Nevada. My father, Benjamin Munkers, was among them. His family was composed of an invalid wife, three married sons and one married daughter, besides five younger children, the youngest a boy of five years. I was then ten years old and still have quite a clear memory of the journey and of conditions of the early days spent in Oregon.

All the way across, Mother was unable to do anything, even having to be lifted in and out of the wagon. She made the entire ride on a bed. It was my work to help brother's wife, who managed the cooking for our camp.

The Munkers family started out with five wagons drawn by oxen; three yoke to each wagon, thirty head of oxen, fifty head of roan Durham cows and five saddle horses. These made up our herd. Most all the company drove through some stock but I think no other family had so many as we.

When we left Missouri, there was a train of about one hundred wagons but that was found to be too large a party to travel together as the teams must be kept up by grazing by the way. So they scattered out under leaders or train captains, as we called them. When we started, a man by the name of Martin was our Captain. Later when our train was much smaller, Ben Simpson, father of Sam L. Simpson, was our head man. The future Poet of Oregon was then Baby Sam of the camp. Many a time I cared for him while his mother was doing the family wash.

After we left Missouri, all the buildings I remember seeing were Forts Laramie, Bridges and Hall. As this was but the second year of "Crossing the Plains", the way before us was much of it through a wilderness and over a trackless plain. There were no bridges, no ferries and a stream too large to be forded was crossed by means of rafts, if there could be found timber along its banks to make rafts. If not, our wagon beds were used for flat boats.

We had no trouble with the Indians but we did have one awful scare. It was when we were in Utah. All at once our train seemed to be surrounded on all sides by mounted Indians! It was a war party going out to fight another tribe. I do believe there were ten thousand of them and we thought it was the last of us, but when they had seen us all they wanted to, they gave a whoop and a yell and away they clattered!

Of those long weary months I cannot clearly tell. I know it was April when we started and October when we reached the place that was to be our home in Oregon. Sometimes we stopped several days in camp where we found plenty of water and good grazing and while the teams rested and fed up, the men fixed up the wagons and helped the women wash and prepare food for the next drive ahead. Then there were days we toiled over the arid plains till far into the night to reach the life-giving water that was a necessity to us and to our trains. The children of the company walked many many miles. . . . sometimes I think I walked half of the way to

Oregon! Some days it was very hard to find fuel enough for our camp fires. Many a time our simple meals were cooked over a fire of buffalo chips and sage brush. The weather did not cause as much trouble. I recall but one real storm. It was on the Platte River in Nebraska. We were in camp on the bank of the river when it came on. The wind blew a hurricane! Thunder roared and lightening flashed! It was a dark as Egypt. The rain poured like it was being emptied from buckets. I will never forget that night! Every tent was blown down. No one was seriously hurt, though a babe was narrowly missed by a falling tent pole. The men chained the wagons together to hold them from being blown into the river. Our camp belongings were blown helter skelter over the country around about and our stock was stampeded 'till it took all the next day to get them rounded up.

But after all, we had but few hardships compared with some of the emigrant trains. Some years, you know, there was Cholera that wiped out entire families and trains that were raided by Indians and too, there were times when the oxen were diseased and died leaving families stranded on the plains. Yes, we were very lucky!

In the early Autumn we reached the Columbia River and we drove down through the Barlow Pass and came into the Willamette Valley. We made camp there where the Swartz place is now. Father was anxious to secure a place where he could have shelter for the invalid mother and when he found a chance to buy out a homesteader (a man by the name of Anderson) he was glad to pay him his price ($1000) and take possession at once. The place was on Mill Creek, four miles East of Salem. There was a comfortable log house of two rooms, a log barn and ten of the 640 acres was farmed. Thus, before the winter rains came on we were snugly settled. Father brought in what supplies he could for the house and for our stock, but most of the cattle were turned on the range. The first winter's work was making rails with which to fence the farm. Then followed sod breaking and seeding, thus adding some acres each year to our fields. Father set out an orchard of apple and peach trees in the spring of 1850, I think it was. I don't remember where he got the nursery stock.

He brought a half bushel of peach stones from Missouri. The orchard grew nicely and I think it was in the autumn of 1855 that father had 100 bushels of apples to sell. Fourteen dollars was the price he got per bushel. I do not often hear it spoken of now, but there was a time in the settlement where we lived when peas and wheat were currency. I cannot now say what the face value was, but I think one bushel either represented $1.00 in debit or credit. Peas were much used for coffee and often the only sweetening to be had was molasses.

Oh no, we were not poor! Father brought $10,000 to this country. How? In gold and silver. You know mother was brought on a bedstead set right into the wagon. Well, underneath her bed was a box of bedding and in that box, the money was cached. Yes, we soon had pretty good homes started but the stampede to the gold mines in California in 1849–50 was a bad thing for our families. Four of my brothers went (Thomas, 14 years old / Ben, 16 years old / Riley, 19 years old and Marion). Marion later died there. They would all have gotten ahead faster had they stayed home.

Where did I go to school? I did not have much chance to go to school after we came here. One winter the neighbors got up a school. There was a vacant house and they hired a man to teach the children awhile. I went. That was about all the schooling I had after I came to Oregon. Yes, I've been here a long time. Seventy years! I've seen Oregon grow up!

What became of those who crossed the plains in our train? Well, the Crowleys settled in Polk County and the Fullerson's also as well as Glenn Burnett, our train preacher. The Browns, the Blakelys the Finleys and the Kirks settled in Linn County. Ben Simpson and family lived in Salem. Yes, I know most all the old timers. L. F. Grover, afterward Governor of Oregon and US Senator, was a guest at my wedding. Reverend Roberts, one of the early pioneers of Methodism performed the ceremony.

Do I remember the hard winter and the great flood of 1861 & 1862? Yes! What was the worst winter and the greatest flood in all the years I've lived here. Much of Salem was under water. The Court House was full of people who had been driven from their homes. Near the old Bennett house, the water was swimming to a horse. The Willamette was a mighty river . . . miles in width, sweeping houses, barns, bridges and everything in its course. No, of course the river hadn't been bridged then, but then all the small streams were adding wreckage to the Willamette. The flood was in December '61. In January came the deep snow which lasted for six weeks and pretty nearly finished what the flood had left.

SKETCH OF HARDSHIPS ENDURED BY THOSE WHO CROSSED THE PLAINS IN '46

David Campbell, 1899

> *David Campbell was in his seventies when he wrote this account of his overland journey on the Oregon Trail for the* Porterville Weekly Review, *in Porterville, California. His encounters with the ill-fated Donner Party and his experiences in California during the earliest days of the fight for statehood make his reminiscence fascinating reading.*

There were 250 wagons in rendezvous at Independence, Mo., ready to start for California on April I, 1846.

In order to guard against Indian raids we organized, divided, into companies of twenty-five to thirty wagons, each company electing its own captain. We then elected Col. William Russell of Kentucky as commander.

We left Independence April 2, 1846. The order given was to start with 250 wagons. Each captain had to furnish four men from his company to stand guard at night, the company that was in the rear at night having to take the lead the next morning, but we soon found this plan would not do, for it made it too late getting into camp. So we concluded that it would be best for each company to be independent and yet keep as near together as possible. Each wagon had from two to three yoke of oxen. In a short time the most of the companies divided up—some of the men wanted to rush through while others favored the more sensible plan of traveling without too much haste. The party which hurried on soon found that their cattle could not stand it, for by the time they had reached the Platte River their cattle were tender-footed and gave out. The company that I was in made it a rule that if they could find a suitable place to camp they would always lay over one day in every week in order to rest up and do their washing. We aimed to travel twelve miles each day stopping when a good camping place was found.

We had to burn "buffalo chips" instead of wood. There were a great many buffaloes on the plains at that time. They run in bands and we would hardly ever be out of sight of a band of from 100 to 1000 of these magnificent animals. It was fine sport shooting them as they ran. There were four of us who had nothing else to do but hunt, viz: Green Patterson, John Foster, David Wray and myself, and we were very successful in killing the buffalo. The way we managed to get them was to station three men out to one side and not let the buffalo see them—this was easy to do as the country was rolling—and then one would go around and start them in the direction of the men laying in wait and as they passed the men would select a fine one and shoot him. If the animal was only crippled he would turn and make for the smoke of the gun; in that case all we had to do was to jump to one side and put in another shot. I have put in as many as five shots that way before succeeding in killing some of them. There would be from five to ten killed each day. We had all the buffalo and antelope we wanted. The buffalo is very clumsy and runs like a cow. A horse will run on to one very quickly. When one of them starts to run he will go one way and you can't turn him, but have to get out of the way. We had to be on our guard to keep them from stampeding our stock.

By the time the companies that were trying to rush through had reached Fort Laramie their stock gave out, but they found traders there, so they traded their oxen off for others, and before we got to Fort Hall they were in the rear.

We were out of buffalo range when we struck the Rocky Mountains, but we found plenty of mountain sheep, or goats some people call them. They were fine eating. They, too, went in bands ranging from 1000 to 3000 inhabited the roughest places in the mountains, going with ease over places where a man could not walk. They had very large horns which seemed to be quite useful to them at times and especially so when they jumped from one cliff to another, for they would always light on their heads. One time I was slipping around a cliff of rocks and I came upon a band of kids under a large shelving rock, the band numbering at least 200, and it was fine sport picking them up and watching them run in every direction.

There were a great many wolves in the Rocky Mountains at that time. They were very large and white; they would come around our camp at night and bark

We had a great many large streams to cross, but fortunately the rivers were all very low that year and the streams between Independence and Sutter's Fort were all forded without getting anything in the wagons wet and that without having to prop up the wagon beds.

We traveled up Sweet River for two days; the beaver dams were thick on the river and the mountains on each side of it were capped with snow. This brought us up to the Devil's Gate, where we laid over one day to view the grand scenery. The river made a short turn here and left the valley and came rushing down a narrow pass some 500 feet, with solid rock on both sides, the channel being about fifty feet wide. This brought us on the waters of the Pacific slope. Bear River was also a beautiful stream and was full of large mountain trout. When we reached the Steam Boat Spring we laid over a day to fish and enjoy the grandeur that surrounded us. The water in the spring was boiling and threw up steam some twenty feet high and would cook a piece of meat in just a few minutes. It was close to the river bank and the mountains came up close to the spring and the rocks for a mile around looked as if they had been thrown out of a burning pit. They looked like burned cinders. Some of the company thought that was surely the Devil's regions. It was indeed a grand sight to see.

When we arrived at Fort Hall we found about 500 Indians of the Flathead tribe who had come in to trade. They had buffalo hides and deer skins and would pay any price for beads and tobacco. We bought some buffalo robes and I bought a horse for five pounds of tobacco and a pound of beads. I afterwards sold this horse to the Government for $50.00. We found this tribe of Indians very friendly.

After we left Fort Hall the mountain fever began to rage among the members of the party and as there was no doctor in any of the companies a great many of the people died. So, by the time we arrived at Goose Creek, where the Oregon road turned off, about fifty wagons concluded they would go to Oregon, as they had so many deaths in their families.

The Donner party concluded they would take another road, which was called the Hastings cut off, by the way of Fort Bridger. This road proved to be a longer and worse road. The two roads came together again at the foot of the Sierra Nevada Mountains. The Donner party were to put up a notice when they got there, but the company I was in got there two weeks before they did. For some reason they got to quarreling and their captain killed a member of the company and they gave him twelve hours in which to leave the party. William McCutchen and Mr. Eddy left the company with him overtaking our party forty miles from Sutter's Fort. The remainder of the Donner party got to the foot of the mountain, but the storm came on and they could not get any farther. The families of the three men named above were with the Donner party and they were all saved. William McCutchen and the captain that was run off were members of the second party which went to their rescue in the spring.

They made an attempt to go to them in the winter, but they could not get their Indian pilot to go through with them, so it was abandoned for the time.

Our company had a good road most of the way considering the fact that it was a mountain road and had never been worked. Those who came to California bore to the south and came into what is known as the "1000 Spring Valley," a level valley and surrounded by mountains. There were large holes of water every few rods all over the valley, the water being as clear as crystal. They were from five to ten feet across and the water was about one foot below the surface of the ground and they never run over. The ground would shake when a person walked over it. We could not see the bottom of them. I tried to touch bottom with a ten foot pole, but couldn't do it.

We had to guard our stock to keep them from getting into these holes. There were a few willows growing in this valley.

Just after leaving 1000 Spring Valley we struck the head of the Humboldt River. Here we came in contact with hostile Indians, the first we encountered on the trip. We traveled down the river for several days. There were thick willows and good grass all the way down, but the water was bad. We had only one rain on us during the whole trip across the plains.

When we buried our dead we had to bury them in the corral and let the stock tramp everything down so the Indians would not find the place, for they would dig it up for the cloth the body was wrapped in. Three of our men were killed by the Indians. They used poisoned arrows and when shot by one of them the poison would go all through one's system. The Indians would hide in the willows, and shoot arrows in our stock. We had to corral our stock every night and guard them while they were feeding. When we got to the "sinks" of this river we found that we had a desert of thirty-five miles to cross without water or grass. We started in the evening and traveled all night, reaching the Truckee River the next evening.

This is a beautiful river and there was plenty of grass for the stock. We traveled down this river for two days and crossed and recrossed it twenty-five times. We then left the river and bore to the west. This brought us into the mountains where we found we had a very rough country to travel over. When we came to the foot of the Sierra Nevada Mountains it looked as though we could not get farther, but as we had no time to lose we double teamed and took one wagon at a time up to the summit. It was so rocky that we had to work our way around the rocks, and only got a short distance in two days travel. We had a rocky road to travel over after we got up the mountain, but it was not very steep until we got to Boca Creek where we had to chain a tree to the wagons in order to get down the hill safely. This was the steepest hill we had on the whole trip. After we got down to the creek we had to stop and grade a road to get up the hill. There were two companies and it took us three days to complete the grade. This brought us to a dividing ridge which we followed down to the North Fork of the American River, a distance of fifty miles. By this time a good many of the company were out of flour, so they started myself and another man to Johnson's place to get flour. We got 100 pounds and started back to the company.

The captain of the Donner party and Mr Eddy, the man who left with him when he was driven off, overtook us about thirty miles from Johnson's and told us what had happened, and that he had been driven off and were fearful lest the party would never get through as the road was so bad

Our company reached Johnson's place all right and in good spirits. We laid over there two days. While there we heard that the American fleet had landed and hoisted the American flag over the capitol and also at Los Angeles.

From here we started for Sutter's Fort, a distance of fifty miles. There was no road but it was a level country. When we reached Sutter's Fort we laid over there several days, bringing the time up to the 10th of October, making a six months journey from Independence, Missouri

The first American child born in California was born the next day after we arrived at Sutters Fort. They named the child John Sutter Whisman. He is now living in Oregon.

Sutter had two flour mills running to supply the immigrants with flour. This flour was coarse and had not been bolted. The mills were built in cheap style. They used two stones with a lever attached and a squaw would turn the lever around. We got fine beef. They were only worth what the hide and tallow would bring. A large beef was valued at five dollars. After being here five days the immigrants divided up, some going to Napa County and others going to Santa Clara County. Just before we all separated Lieut. Blackburn came up from Monterey as a recruiting officer for Col. Fremont to enlist men to join his regiment going to Lower California, where the American flag had been pulled down and the Spanish flag hoisted instead. All of the men who could go enlisted and their families were ordered to go to Santa Clara Mission, where they could be guarded and have houses to live in. Col. Fremont commissioned Capt. Arom to raise a company and guard the women and children. The Government gave to each woman and child a soldier's ration.

The most of the men that Blackburn enlisted went down with him to Monterey. I could not get ready to go with him and so he arranged for me to be at San Jose by November 1st, to meet Capt. Buress, who was getting horses for Col. Fremont. He had 500 horses and saddles. There were fifty men in the company to guard and drive the horses. When we got to the Salinas plains the Spanish were hidden in the brush and had cut off our advance guard, and commenced shooting at us. They got behind trees the best they could in order to protect themselves. There were six advance guards; one was killed and two were wounded. There were two hundred of the Spaniards. Capt. Buress went to the rescue as soon as possible. He gave orders for twenty men to run the horses to Gomez' corral and to guard them there. This was a distance of two miles. Capt. Buress gave orders to the thirty remaining men to examine their guns and then follow him. The Spaniards left our guard and formed in line and when we got within about three hundred yards of them they fired on us. The Captain then ordered his men to dismount and fire and then ordered them to remount and charge, and when the charge was made the Spanish scattered in every direction. During this charge Captain Buress' horse ran away with him, taking him right among the Spanish and they speared him to death. Our loss was only five, the Spaniards lost eighteen and we held the ground. They were allowed to bury their own dead the next day.

Col. Fremont dispatched Lieut. Blackburn to San Jose with a cannon and ten men. I was in this party and when we got to San Jose I had to be left there under Capt. Webber on account of sickness in our family. This is how I happened to get into the Santa Clara battle, January, 1847. There were twenty-five Spaniards raised against the American flag and they hoisted their own flag. They were in rendezvous near what we call Half Moon Bay. They were commanded by Schanres, who had been paroled. Captain Webber found where they had been encamped and they only had sixty men in their company. He notified Lieut. Maddix, who had a company of fifty rangers, to be at a certain place on a certain day. He also notified Captain Mardson, who was captain of the marines at Urbano, which is now called Presidio. He came up with a cannon and one hundred men on foot. Mardson ranked in office, so both of the other men had to submit to his orders.

By this time the Spaniards had moved camp to within three miles of Santa Clara Mission where the women and children were living. They were guarded by Capt. Arom. He could not leave his post so he put up breastworks to keep them from getting to the houses and for his men to fight behind. The Spaniards were camped in full view of the Mission. The people at the Mission expected every hour to be attacked, but they were there three days when our soldiers came upon them. Captain Webber came up on the north of them and Capt. Maddix on the south and got between them and the Mission. Mardson was behind them with his marines and cannon. The Spaniards advanced toward the Mission across a mud slough which was a half mile wide. When Mardson got into that they commenced firing at him, and he could not use the cannon on account of the mud, and as the Spaniards would not get within 300 yards of his men they could not hit a man. Capt. Webber and Lieut. Maddix charged on them but the Spaniards kept too far away and they could not do them much damage. They killed three Spaniards and wounded several. One American was shot in the leg. The fight lasted three hours, and at night the Spaniards retreated to their camp. The next morning they sent in a flag of truce. Capt. Mardson was the highest in rank so he had to treat with them. They parleyed for three days trying to come to terms. They had run all of the horses off which they had taken from the Americans and had hidden all of their good guns, then they were willing to come to terms, but they had to stack all of their arms and give up all of the horses they had taken. They were to drive everything in and let the Americans take their pick. They had over fifty head. The Americans gave up all of theirs. Capt. Webber hired a Spanish cart to haul our saddles and blankets to San Jose. We never left the barracks any more until we were discharged, which was one month later.

Now as to the hardships the pioneer had to encounter ill California in 1846. During the war everything an American owned had to be guarded, as the Spaniards would steal anything they could get hold of, and it was dangerous for a man to go out alone.

The emigrants put in a crop of wheat on the Mission land. While putting in the crop it was necessary for four or five men to go together and have one stand guard. Peace was declared in 1847, but it did not make matters any better. We were under a military government and Spanish law in force but it did not amount to much. Everything was tried before the Alcade. The governor appointed him and whatever he said had to be done. In one Instance the Priest complained to the Alcade that the Americans were tresspassing on the Mission land, which was five miles square, and he wanted them driven off. The Alcade ordered them off but they refused to go and the Alcade then called on the governor for assistance and he sent soldiers, who drove the men off; when the soldiers were gone, however, they went back. This was government land.

In 1847 there were two Americans shot and one lost and dragged to death. I saw an American taken up before the Alcade and tried for stealing. The Alcalde ordered him tied to a post and given thirty lashes and sold for thirty days to the highest bidder, the latter part of the penalty being imposed for the purpose of getting money to pay the costs. It was a great day of rejoicing when in 1850 we were admitted into the Union and to be governed by our own laws.

In 1848 the first gold was discovered by Mr. Marshall where Captain Sutter was building a saw mill. They did not know whether it was gold or not, but thought it was something very valuable, so they sent a man in poste haste down to Monterey with it to Governor Mason to find out what it was. He told him it was gold, and he showed the sample in San Jose as he passed through and said the ground was full of it. That started the rush and the news flew fast all over the world. The San Joaquin River was so high we could not get within three miles of it, so we had to go by way of Benicia and cross the Bay on an old flat boat which was worked by oars. This boat could make but one trip a day on account of the tide being up and down, so those wishing to cross had to wait for their turn. When I reached there I was told I would have to wait three weeks before my urn would come. There were two other men with me and they were old sea captains and understood all about a boat, so we got a skiff there and put our saddles and camping outfit in the skiff, then tied two of our horses to it and the other two we held close to the boat and one of us rowed the boat across the Bay, a distance of three-quarters of a mile. We kept the horses heads out of the water and they floated over all right. This was the first time horses were ever swam across the Bay at Benecia. We then started for the Fort, crossing the Sacramento on a boat, and went to Morman Island on the American River. We found about fifty men at work with rockers.

We had with us a hand-saw, draw-knife, hatchet, pick and shovel; this was our completeoutfit. We got a hollow log, cut it off about four feet long and made us a rocker and went to work on the island. One of the men did the rocking, another threw in the gravel and the third man poured in water to wash the gravel. In this way we made one and a third ounces each day as long as we stayed in the mines. The weather got so hot we concluded we would go back to San Jose and complete the saw mill I was building when the mining fever broke out. This was the first saw mill built in Santa Clara County. When we had finished the mill we went back to the mines. The first of September we went to the place which is now called Placerville. The gold here was very coarse. The only tools we used in getting It out were a pick, spoon, butcher knife and pan. I stayed there three weeks and averaged fifty dollars per day for that time

One of our party was taken sick with the mountain fever, so I had to put him into a wagon and take him to San Jose, and when I got there I concluded to go to work In my saw mill instead of going back to the mines. I commenced making lumber and sold it at $50.00 per thousand. I kept raising on the price, and in 1849 it went up to $300.00 per thousand at the mill and everything else was high in proportion. Flour sold at $30.00 per barrel. In 1849 everything was booming in San Jose.

There were only five houses in San Francisco n 1847; the customs house, post-office, Leigdoff's store and a tavern kept by Mr. Bennett. There was not a wharf in the place until the fall of 1847. Mr. Clark, a man who crossed the plains with me put up the first wharf, running it out from Clark's Point which was named for him. The first town lots were laid off in 1847. They made the streets only eighty feet wide, but in 1850 they found the streets were too narrow, so they moved the buildings back twenty feet on the main streets. One can hardly believe that there could be such a change made in fifty-two years. San Jose was an old Spanish town. In the fall of 1847 the Alcalde issued a proclamation calling all the citizens together who were living on the town land, to survey off the town into lots and to release the remainder of the land that belonged to the town under the Spanish law. So they found there were forty families entitled to land. They surveyed it off in five acre tracts and gave each one a lease for ninety-nine years. This is called the San Jose forty thieves, but being done under the Spanish law the title is good. I helped to survey the town in 1847. The main street is one hundred feet wide and the others are eighty feet. At this time there were no Americans living in San Jose except a few who had been there for twenty years and had Spanish families. The Alcalde was a shrewd Englishman and was appointed by the governor.

I understand there is a dispute in regard to the first sermon that was preached in California. History gives it as being in 1847, by Rev. Mr. Roberts, who was on his way to Oregon as a missionary. He preached a sermon at that time in San Francisco. But in December, 1846, there was a local Methodist preacher, who crossed the plains with us, preached a funeral sermon over the remains of the daughter of Captain Arom, who died just before Christmas. There were about fifty people present at this funeral. I was present and heard this sermon in 1846. The minister's name was Heacock. The sermon was preached in old Santa Clara Mission.

(Signed) David Campbell

THE DIARY OF PATRICK BREEN, ONE OF THE DONNER PARTY, NOVEMBER 1846 TO MARCH 1847

Few diaries kept on the trail are as poignant as the one kept by Patrick Breen during the months he and the rest of the Donner Party were stranded by high snows in the Sierra Nevada, near the end of their journey to California.

Nov. 1846

Friday Nov. 20th 1846. Came to this place on the 31st of 1846 last month that it snowed we went on to the pass the snow so deep we were unable to find the road, when within 3 miles of the summit then turned back to this shanty on the Lake, Stanton came one day after we arriveed here we again took our teams & waggons & made another unsuccessful attempt to cross in company with Stanton we returned to the shanty it continueing to snow all the time we were here we now have killed most part of our cattle having to stay here untill next spring & live on poor beef without bread or salt it snowed during the space of eight days with little intermission, after our arrival here, the remainder of time up to this day was clear & pleasant frezeing at night the snow nearly gone from the valleys.

Sat. 21st Fine morning wind N:W 22 of our company are about starting across the mountain this moring including Stanton & his indians, some clouds flying thawed to day wnd E.

Sunday 22nd Froze hard last night this a fine clear morning wind E.S.E no account from those on the mountains.

Monday 23rd Same weather wind W the expedition across the mountains returned after an unsucesful attempt.

Tuesday 24th Fine in the morning towards eveng cloudy & windy wind W looks like snow freezeing hard.

Wendsday 25th Wind about W N W Cloudy looks like the eve of a snow storm our mountainers intend trying to cross the mountain tomorrow if fair froze hard last night.

Thurssday the 26th Began to snow yesterday in the evening now rains or sleet the mountaniers dont start to day the wind about W. wet & muddy.

Friday 27 Continues to snow, the ground not covered, Wind W dull prospect for crossing the mountains.

Saturday 28th Snowing fast now about 10 o clock snow 8 or 10 inches deep soft wet snow, weather not cold wind W.

Sunday 29th Still snowing now about 3 feet deep, wind W killed my last oxen to day will skin them tomorrow gave another yoke to Fosters hard to get wood.

Monday 30th Snowing fast wind W about 4 or 5 feet deep, no drifts looks as likely to continue as when it commenced no liveing thing without wings can get about.

Dec. 1846

December 1st Tuesday Still snowing wind W snow about 5½ feet or 6 deep difficult to get wood no going from the house completely housed up looks as likely for snow as when it commenced, our cattle all killed but three or four them, the horses & Stantons mules gone & cattle suppose lost in the snow no hopes of finding them alive.

Wedns. 2nd. Continues to snow wind W sun shineing hazily thro the clouds dont snow quite as fast as it has done snow must be over six feet deep bad fire this morning.

Thursd. 3rd Snowed a little last night bright and cloudy at intervals all night, to day cloudy snows none wind S.W. warm but not enough so to thaw snow lying deep allround expecing it to thaw a little to day the forgoing written in the morning it immediately turned in to snow & continued to snow all day & likely to do so all night.

Friday 4th Cloudy that is flying clouds neither snow or rain this day it is a relief to have one fine day, wind E by N no sign of thaw freezeing pretty hard snow deep.

Saturday 5th Fine clear day beautiful sunshine thawing a little looks delightful after the long snow storm.

Sund. 6th The morning fine & clear now some cloudy wind S-E not much in the sunshine, Stanton & Grave, manufactureing snow shoes for another mountain scrabble no account of mules.

Mond. 7th Beautiful clear day wind E by S looks as if we might some fair weather no thaw.

Tues 8th Fine weather Clear & pleasant froze hard last night wind S.E deep snow the people not stiring round much hard work to wood sufficient to keep us warm cook our beef.

Wedns. 9th Commenced snowing about 11 o clock wind N:W snows fast took in Spitzer yesterday so weak that he cannot rise without help caused by starveation all in good health some having scant supply of beef Stanton trying to make a raise of some for his Indians & self not likely to get much.

Thursd. 10th Snowed fast all night with heavy squalls of wind Continues still to snow the sun peeping through the clouds once in about three hours very difficult to get wood to day now about 2 o clock looks likely to continue snowing dont know the debth of the snow may be 7 feet.

Friday 11th Snowing a little wind W sun vissible at times not freezeing.

Satd. 12th Continues to snow wind W weather mild freezeind little.

Sunday 13th Snows faster than any previous day wind N:W Stanton & Graves with several others makeing preperations to cross the mountains on snow shoes, snow 8 feet deep on the level dull.

Monday 14 Fine morning sunshine cleared off last night about 12 o clock wind E:S:E dont thaw much but fair for a continueance of fair weather.

Tuesday 15th Still continues fine wind W:S:W.

Wed'd 16th Fair & pleasant froeze hard last night so the company started on snow shoes to cross the mountains wind S.E looks pleasant.

Thursd. 17th Pleasant sunshine to day wind about S.E Bill Murp returned from the mountain party last evening Bealis died night before last Milt. & Noah went to Donnos 8 days since not returned yet, thinks they got lost in the snow. J Denton here to day.

Frid'd. 18 Beautiful day sky clear it would be delightful were it not for the snow lying so deep thaws but little on the south side of shanty saw no strangers to day from any of the shantys.

Satd. 19 Snowd. last night commenced about 11 o clock. Squalls of wind with snow at intervals this morning thawing wind. N by W a little singular for a thaw may continue, it continues to snow sunshining cleared off towards evening.

Sund. 20 Night clear froze a little now clear & pleasant wind N W thawing a little Mrs Reid here, no account of Milt. yet Dutch Charley started for Donoghs turned back not able to proceed tough times, but not discouraged our hopes are in God. Amen.

Mond. 21 Milt. got back last night from Donos camp sad news. Jake Donno Sam Shoemaker Rinehart, & Smith are dead the rest of them in a low situation Snowed all night with a strong S-W wind to day cloudy wind continues but not snowing, thawing sun shineing dimly in hopes it will clear off.

Tuesd. 22nd Snowd. all last night Continued to snow all day with some few intermissions had a severe fit of the gravel yesterday I am well to day, Praise be to the God of Heaven.

Wend. 23rd Snowd. a little last night clear to day & thawing a little. Milt took some of his meat to day all well at their camp began this day to read the Thirty days prayer, may Almighty God grant the request of an unworthy sinner that I am. Amen.

Thursd. 24th Rained all night & still continues to rain poor prospect for any kind of comfort spiritual or temporal, wind S: may God help us to spend the Christmass as we ought considering circumstances.

Friday 25th Began to snow yesterday about 12 o clock snowd. all night & snows yet rapidly wind about E by N Great difficulty in geting wood John & Edwd. has to get I am not able offerd. our prayers to God this Cherimass morning the prospect is apalling but hope in God Amen.

Satd. 26th Cleared off in the night to day clear & pleasant Snowd. about 20 inches or two feet deep yesterday, the old snow was nearly run soft before it began to snow now it is all soft the top dry & the under wet wind S. E.

Sund. 27th Continues clear froze hard last night Snow very deep say 9 feet thawing a little in the sun scarce of wood to day chopt. a tree dow it sinks in the snow & is hard to be got.

Monday 28th Snowd. last night cleared off this morning snowd. a little now clear & pleasant.

Tuesday 29th Fine clear day froze hard last night. Charley sick. Keysburg has Wolfings Rifle gun.

Wedsd. 30th Fine clear morning froze hard last night Charley died last night about 10 o clock had with him in money $1.50 two good loking silver watches one razor 3 boxes caps Keysburg tok them into his possession Spitzer took his coat & waistcoat Keysburg all his other little effects gold pin one shirt and tools for shaveing.

Thursday 31st Last of the year, may we with Gods help spend the comeing year better than the past which we purpose to do if Almighty God will deliver us from our present dredful situation which is our prayer if the will of God sees it fiting for us Amen. morning fair now cloudy wind E by S for three days past freezeing hard every night looks like another snow storm Snow Storms are dredful to us snow very deep crust on the [under?].

Jan. 1847

Jany. 1st 1847 We pray the God of mercy to deliver us from our present calamity if it be his Holy will Amen. Commencd. snowing last night does not snow fast wind S:E sun peeps out at times provisions geting scant dug up a hide from under the snow yesterday for Milt. did not take it yet.

Sat. 2nd Fair & thawey snow got soft wind S-E looks thawey froze pretty hard last night.

Sund. 3rd Continues fair in day time freezeing at night wind about E Mrs. Reid talks of crossing the mountains with her children provisions scarce.

Mond. 4th Fine morning looks like spring thawing now about 12 oclock wind S:E Mrs. Reid Milt. Virginia & Eliza started about ½ hour ago with prospect of crossing the mountain may God of Mercy help them left ther children here Tom's with us Pat with Keysburg & Jas with Gravese's folks, it was difficult for Mrs Reid to get away from the children.

Tuesd. 5th Beautiful day thawing some in the sun wind S-E snow not settleing much we are in hopes of the rainy time ending.

Weds. 6th Fine day clear not a cloud froze very hard last night wind S:E Eliza came back from the mountain yesterday evening not able to proceed, to day went to Graves, the others kept ahead.

Thursd. 7th Continues fine freezeing hard at night very cold this morning wind S.S.E dont think we will have much more snow snow not thawing much not much dimeinished in debph.

Friday 8th Fine morning wind E froze hard last night very cold this morning Mrs. Reid & company came back this moring could not find their way on the other side of the mountain they have nothing but hides to live on Martha is to stay here Milt. & Eliza going to Donos Mrs. Reid & the 2 boys going to their own shanty & Virginia prospects dull may God relieve us all from this difficulty if it is his Holy will Amen.

Satd 9th Continues fine freezeing hard at night this a beatiful morning wind about S.S.E Mrs. Reid here Virginias toes frozen a little snow settleing none to be perceivd.

Sund. 10 Began to snow last night still continues wind W N W.

Mond. 11th Still continues to snow fast, looks gloomy Mrs Reid at Keysburgs Virg. with us wood scarce difficult to get any more wind W.

Tuesd 12th Snows fast yet new snow about 3 feet deep wind S:W no sign of clearing off.

Wens. 13th Snowing fast wind N.W snow higher than the shanty must be 13 feet deep dont know how to get wood this morning it is dredful to look at.

Thursd. 14th New moon Cleard. off yesterday evening snowd. a little during first part of night Calm but a little air from the North very pleasant to day sun shineing brilliantly renovates our spirits prais be to God, Amen.

Frid. 15th Fine clear day wind N W Mrs. Murphy blind Lanth. not able to get wood has but one axe betwixt him & Keysburg, he moved to Murphys yesterday looks like another storm expecting some account from Siuters soon.

Satd. 16th Wind blew hard all night from the W. abated a little did not freeze much this is clear & pleasant wind a little S of W no telling what the weather will do.

Sund. 17th Fine morning sun shineing clear wind S.S.E Eliza came here this morning, sent her back again to Graves Lanthrom crazy last night so Bill says, Keyburg sent Bill to get hides off his shanty & carry thim home this morning, provisions scarce hides are the only article we depend on, we have a little meat yet, may God send us help.

Mond. 18th Fine day clear & pleasant wind W, thawing in the sun Mrs. Murphy here to day very hard to get wood.

Tuesd. 19th Clear & pleasant thawing a little in the Sun wind S.W Peggy & Edward sick last night by eating some meat that Dolan threw his tobacco on, pretty well to day (praise God for his blessings,) Lanthrom very low in danger if relief dont soon come hides are all the go, not much of any other in camp.

Wed. 20th Fine morning wind N froze hard last night. Expecting some person across the mountain this week.

Thursd. 21 Fine morning wind W did not freze quite so hard last night as it has done, John Battice & Denton came this morning with Eliza she wont eat hides Mrs Reid sent her back to live or die on them. Milt. got his toes froze the Donoghs are all well.

Frid. 22nd Began to snow a little after sunrise likely to snow a good dale wind W came up very suddenly, now 10 oclock.

Satd. 23rd Blew hard & snowd. all night the most severe storm we experienced this winter wind W sun now 12 oclock peeps out.

Sund. 24th Some cloudy this morning ceased snowing Yesterday about 2 oclock. Wind about S. E all in good health thanks be to God for his mercies endureth for ever, heard nothing from Murphys camp since the storm expet to hear they sufferd some.

Mod 25th Began to snow yesterday evening & Still continues wind W.

Tuesd 26 Cleared up yesterday to day fine & pleasant, wind S. in hopes we are done with snow storms, those that went to Suitors not yet returned provisions geting very scant people geting weak liveing on short allowance of hides.

Weds 27th Began to snow yesterday & still continues to sleet thawing a little wind W Mrs. Keyber here this morning Lewis Suitor she says died three days ago Keysburg sick & Lanthrom. lying in bed the whole of his time dont have fire enough to cook their hides. Bill & Sim. Murphy sick.

Thursd. 28th Full moon cleared off last night & froze some to day fine & warm wind S.E looks some like spring weather birds chirping qute lively full moon today.

Frid 29th Fine morning began to thaw in the sun early. wind S.W froze hard last night there will be a crust soon God send Amen.

Satd. 30th Fine pleasant morning wind W begining to thaw in the sun John & Edwd. went to Graves this morning the Graves seized on Mrs Reids goods untill they would be paid also took the hides that she &

family had to live on, she got two peices of hides from there & the ballance they have taken you may know from these proceedings what our fare is in camp there is nothing to be got by hunting yet perhaps there soon will. God send it Amen.

Sund. 31st. The sun dont shine out brilliant this morning froze prtty hard last night wind N.W. Lantron Murphy died last night about I o clock, Mrs. Reid & John went to Graves this morning to look after her goods.

Feb. 1847

Mond. February the 1st Froze very hard last night cold to day & cloudy wind N W. sun shines dimly the snow has not settled much John is unwell to day with the help of God & he will be well by night Amen.

Tuesday 2nd Began to snow this morning & continued to snow untill night now clear wind during the storm S. W.

Wend. 3rd Cloudy looks like more snow not cold, froze a little last night wind S.S W. it was clear all last night sun shines out at times.

Thurd. 4th Snowd. hard all night & still continues with a strong S: W. wind untill now abated looks as if it would snow all day snowd. about 2 feet deep now.

Frid. 5th Snowd. hard all untill 12 o'clock at night wind still continud to blow hard from the S. W: to day pretty clear a few clouds only Peggy very uneasy for fear we shall all perrish with hunger we have but a little meat left & only part of 3 hides has to support Mrs. Reid she has nothing left but one hide & it is on Graves shanty Milt is livig there & likely will keep that hide Eddys child died last night.

Satd. 6th It snowd. faster last night & to day than it has done this winter & still continues without an intermission wind S. W Murphys folks or Keysburgs say they cant eat hides I wish we had enough of them Mrs Eddy very weak.

Sund. 7th Ceasd. to snow last after one of the most severe storms we experienced this winter the snow fell about 4 feet deep. I had to shovel the snow off our shanty this morning it thawd so fast & thawd. during the whole storm. to day it is quite pleasant wind S. W. Milt here to day says Mrs Reid has to get a hide from Mrs. Murphy & McCutchins child died 2nd of this month.

Mond. 8th Fine clear morning wind S. W. froze hard last. Spitzer died last night about 3 o clock to we will bury him in the snow Mrs Eddy died on the night of the 7th.

Tuesd. 9th. Mrs. Murphy here this morning Pikes child all but dead Milt at Murphys not able to get out of bed Keyburg never gets up says he is not able. John went down to day to bury Mrs Eddy & child heard nothing from Graves for 2 or 3 days Mrs Murphy just now going to Graves fine moring wind S. E. froze hard last night begins to thaw in the sun.

Wednsd. 10th Beautiful morning wind W: froze hard last night, to day thawing in the sun Milt Elliot died las night at Murphys shanty about 9 o'clock P: M: Mrs Reid went there this morning to see after his effects. J Denton trying to borrow meat for Graves had none to give they have nothing but hides all are entirely out of meat but a little we have our hides are nearly all eat up but with Gods help spring will soon smile upon us.

Thursd 11th Fine morning wind W. froze hard last night some clouds lying in the E: looks like thaw John Denton here last night very delicate. John & Mrs Reid went to Graves this morning.

Frid. 12th A warm thawey morning wind S. E. we hope with the assistance of Almighty God to be able to live to see the bare surface of the earth once more. O God of Mercy grant it if it be thy holy will Amen.

Sat. 13th Fine morning clouded up yesterday evening snowd a little & continued cloudy all night, cleared off about day light wind about S: W Mrs Reid has headacke the rest in health.

Sund 14th Fine morning but cold before the sun got up, now thawing in the sun wind S E Ellen Graves here this morning John Denton not well froze hard last night John & Edwd. E burried Milt. this morning in the snow.

Mond. 15. Moring cloudy untill 9 o clock then cleared off wam & sunshine wind W. Mrs Graves refusd. to give Mrs Reid any hides put Suitors pack hides on her shanty would not let her have them says if I say it will thaw it then will not, she is a case.

Tuesd. 16th Commencd. to rain yesterday evening turned to snow during the night & continud untill after daylight this morning it is now sun shine & light showers of hail at times wind N.W by W. we all feel very weakly to day snow not geting much less in quantity.

Wedsd. 17th Froze hard last night with heavy clouds runing from the N. W. & light showers of hail at times to day same kind of weather wind N. W. very cold & cloudy no sign of much thaw.

Thrsd 18th Froze hard last night to day clear & warm in the sun cold in the shanty or in the shade wind S. E all in good health Thanks be to Almighty God Amen.

Frid. 19th Froze hard last night 7 men arrived from Colifornia yesterday evening with som provisions but left the greater part on the way to day clear & warm for this region some of the men are gone to day to Donnos Camp will start back on Monday.

Saturd. 20th Pleasant weather.

Sund 21st Thawey warm day.

Mond 22nd The Californians started this morning 24 in number some in a very weak state fine morning wind S. W. for the 3 last days Mrs Keyburg started & left Keysburg here unable to go I burried Pikes child this moring in the snow it died 2 days ago, Paddy Reid & Thos. came back Messrs Graves & Mutry.

Tuesd. 23 Froze hard last night to day fine & thawey has the appearance of spring all but the deep snow wind S:S.E. shot Towser to day & dressed his flesh Mrs Graves came here this morning to borrow meat dog or ox they think I have meat to spare but I know to the contrary they have plenty hides I live principally on the same.

Wend. 24th Froze hard last night to day cloudy looks like a storm wind blows hard from the W. Commenced thawing there has not any more returned from those who started to cross the mts.

Thursd. 25th Froze hard last night fine & sunshiny to day wind W. Mrs Murphy says the wolves are about to dig up the dead bodies at her shanty, the nights are too cold to watch them, we hear them howl.

Frid 26th Froze hard last night today clear & warm Wind S: E: blowing briskly Marthas jaw swelled with the toothache; hungry times in camp, plenty hides but the folks will not eat them we eat them with a tolerable good apetite. Thanks be to Almighty God. Amen Mrs Murphy said here yesterday that thought she would commence on Milt. & eat him. I dont that she has done so yet, it is distressing The Donnos told the California folks that they commence to eat the dead people 4 days ago, if they did not succeed that day or next in finding their cattle then under ten or twelve feet of snow & did not know the spot or near it, I suppose they have done so ere this time.

Satd. 27th Beautiful morning sun shineing brilliantly, wind about S. W. the snow has fell in debth about 5 feet but no thaw but the sun in day time it freezeing hard every night, heard some geese fly over last night saw none.

Sund. 28th Froze hard last night to day fair & sunshine wind S.E. I solitary Indian passed by yesterday come from the lake had a heavy pack on his back gave me 5 or 6 roots resembleing onions in shape taste some like a sweet potatoe. all full of little tough fibres.

Mar. 1847

Mond. March the 1st So fine & pleasant froze hard last night there has 10 men arrived this morning from Bear Valley with provisions we are to start in two or three days & cash our goods here there is amongst them some old they say the snow will be here untill June.

FROM THE *BOOK OF REMINISCENCES,* CALIFORNIA SOCIETY OF PIONEERS

Alvin A. Coffey

> *Alvin Coffey was born a slave in Mason County, Kentucky, in 1822, moving later to Missouri with the family of his owner. He made this journey to California with his owner and earned enough money to buy his own freedom and that of his wife and children, who had remained in Missouri. However, his owner took that money, and decided to return to Missouri with Coffey.*
>
> *Coffey crossed the plains again in 1854 with a new owner and earned seven thousand dollars, with which he freed himself and his wife and children. Coffey prospered in California, as did his family. In California, Coffey home-steaded in Tehama County and was employed by the government while treaties were being established with the Modoc Indians, and at one point had an interest in Sutter's mines.*

I started from St. Louis, Mo., on the 2nd day of April in 1849. There was quite a crowd of the neighbors who drove through the mud and rain to St. Joe to see us off. About the first of May we organized the train. There were twenty wagons in number and from three to five men to each wagon.

We crossed the Missouri River at Savanna Landing on about the sixth of May. There were several trains ahead of us. At twelve o'clock three more men took our place and we went to camp. At six in the morning, there were three more who went to relieve those on guard. One of the three that came in had cholera so bad that he was in lots of misery. Dr. Bassett, the captain of the train, did all he could for him, but he died at ten o'clock and we buried him. We got ready and started at eleven the same day and the moon was new just then.

We got news every day that people were dying by the hundreds in St. Joe and St. Louis. It was alarming. When we hitched up and got ready to move, Dr. said, "Boys, we will have to drive day and night."

There were only three saddle horses in the train, Dr. Bassett, Mr. Hale, Sr., and John Triplet owning them. They rode with the Dr. to hunt camping places. We drove night and day and got out of reach of the cholera. There was none ahead of us that we knew of.

Dave and Ben Headspeth's train was ahead of us. They had fourteen or fifteen wagons in the train and three to five men to a wagon. Captain Camel had another such train. When we caught up with them, we never heard of one case of cholera on their trains.

We got across the plains to Fort Laramie, the sixteenth of June, and the ignorant driver broke down a good many oxen on the trains. There were a good many ahead of us, who had doubled up their trains and left tons upon tons of bacon and other provisions.

When we got well down Humboldt to a place called Lawson's Meadow, which was quite a way from the sink of the Humboldt, the emigrants agreed to drive there. There was good grass at Lawson's Meadow. We camped there a day and two nights, resting the oxen, for we had a desert to cross to get to Black Rock where there was grass and water.

Starting to cross the desert to Black Rock at four o'clock in the evening, we traveled all night. The next day it was hot and sandy. When within twenty miles of Black Rock, we saw it very plainly.

A great number of cattle perished before we got to Black Rock. When about fifteen miles from Black Rock, a team of four oxen was left on the road just where the oxen had died. Everything was left in the wagon.

I drove one oxen all the time and I knew about how much an ox could stand. Between nine and ten o'clock a breeze came up and the oxen threw up their heads and seemed to have new life. At noon, we drove into Black Rock.

Before we reached Sacramento Valley, we had poor feed a number of nights. The route by the way of Humboldt was the oldest and best known to Hangtown. We crossed the South Pass on the Fourth of July. The ice next morning was as thick as a dinner plate. About two days before we got to Honey Lake we were in a timbered country. We camped at a place well known as Rabbit Hole Springs. An ox had given out and was down, and not able to get up, about one hundred yards from the spring. A while after it got dark as it was going to be, the ox commenced bawling pitifully. Some of the boys had gone to bed. I said, "Let us go out and kill the ox for it is too bad to hear him bawl." The wolves were eating him alive. None would go with me, so I got two double-barreled shot-guns which were loaded. I went out where he was. The wolves were not in sight, although I could hear them. I put one of the guns about five or six inches from the ox's head and killed him with the first shot. The wolves never tackled me. I had reserved three shots in case they should.

When we got in Deer Creek in Sacramento Valley, we divided up wagons. Some went to Sacramento Valley to get provisions for the winter and came up to Redding Springs later. We camped several days at Honey Lake but the grass on Madeline Plains was not very good. While Headspeth and a guide we had were hunting the best path to Sacramento road, the cattle recruited up nicely. We took several days to go from Honey Lake to Sacramento Valley.

Those that kept on from Deer Creek to Redding Springs camped at Redding Springs the thirteenth day of October, 1849. Eight to ten miles drive was a big one for us at the latter end. The last four miles the cattle had nothing to eat but poison-oak brush. We cut down black oaks for them to browse on, and got to Redding Springs the next day at four o'clock. We watered the oxen out of buckets that night and morning. The next day we gathered them up, drove them down to Clear Creek where they had plenty of poison oak to eat.

On the morning of the fifteenth we went to dry-digging mining. We dug and dug to the first of November. At night it commenced raining, and rained and snowed pretty much all the winter. We had a tent but it barely kept us all dry. There were from eight to twelve in one camp. We cut down pine trees for shakes to make a cabin. It was a whole week before we had a cabin to keep us dry.

The first week in January, 1850, we bought a hundred pounds of bear meat at one dollar per pound. I asked the man how many pounds he had sold, and he said, "I've sold thirteen hundred pounds and have four hundred to five hundred pounds left in camp yet. I gave the men considerable for helping me dress it.

LETTER WRITTEN ON THE TRAIL TO CALIFORNIA

William Swain

> *Correspondence between those who undertook emigration and their loved ones in the East offers tender glimpses of moments in time on the trail. The journey of William Swain had been a pleasant one, and he had much to reassure his wife with when he wrote to her from the camp celebration on Independence Day, 1849.*

July 4, 1849
in camp for celebration
eight miles below Fort Laramie

Dear Sabrina,

I have just left the celebration dinner table, where the company are now drinking toasts to everything and everybody and cheering at no small rate. I enjoy myself better in conversing with you through the medium of the pen. It is now some time since I wrote home, or at least since I wrote at any length, having written to you a line by a returning emigrant whom I met on the road and had just time to say that we were all well. But there is no certainty in sending letters by such conveyance. You may or may not have received some of the many letters I have sent you by traders and others, on many of which I have paid postage of 25 cents.

. . . We shall pass Fort Laramie tomorrow, where I shall leave this to be take to the States. It will probably be the last time I can write until I get to my journey's end, which may take till the middle of October.

We have had uncommon good health and luck on our route, not having had a case of sickness in the company for the last four weeks. Not a creature has died, not a wagon tire loosened, and no bad luck attended us.

The country is becoming very hilly; the streams rapid, more clear, and assuming the character of mountain streams. The air is very dry and clear, and our path is lined with wild sage and artemisia.

We had a fine celebration today, with an address by Mr. Sexton, which was very good; an excellent dinner, good enough for any hotel; and the boys drank toasts and cheered till they are now going in all sorts around the camp.

I often think of home and all the dear objects of affection there: of George; dear Mother, who was sick; and of yourself and poor little Sister. If it were consistent, I should long for the time to come when I shall turn my footsteps homeward, but such thoughts will not answer now, for I have a long journey yet to complete and then the object of the journey to accomplish.

I am hearty and well, far more so than when I left home. That failing of short breath which troubled me at home has entirely left me. I am also more fleshy. Notwithstanding these facts, I would advise no man to come this way to California.

Give my love to George and Mother and tell them that I am well and enjoy myself. Kiss my little girl for me, and when I get home I will kiss you all.

Your affectionate husband until death,
William Swain

IOWA TO THE "LAND OF GOLD"

Elizabeth Ann McAuley

> *Women who crossed the plains were much involved with domestic duties—ironing, washing, and making sure there was food prepared were all a part of covered wagon life. Still, being a woman emigrant offered opportunities for stretching boundaries, even if it was only in terms of dress, as this diary excerpt shows.*

Wednesday, April 7th, 1852. Bade adiew to home and started amid snow and rain for the land of gold. Our outfit consists of two light strong wagons drawn by oxen and cows, one yoke of heavy oxen for wheelers and a lighter yoke for leaders, with one or two yokes of cows between. We have two saddle horses and a drove of twenty dairy cows, a good sized tent and a sheet iron camp stove which can be set up inside, making it warm and comfortable, no matter what the weather outside.

We have a plentiful supply of provisions, including dried fruits and vegetables, also a quantity of light bread cut into slices and dried for use when it is not convenient to bake. Our stove is furnished with a reflector oven which bakes very nicely. Our clothing is light and durable. My sister and I wear short dresses and bloomers and our foot gear includes a pair of light calf-skin topboots for wading through mud and sand.

Sunday, April 10th. This morning the church bells were calling to worship, but we heeded not their gentle summons and hitching up our teams started onward, leaving church and Sabbath behind us. Road very bad all day. About three o'clock we came to an impassable mud hole in a lane. The only way was to lay down the fence and go through a field. While doing this the owner rushed out in great wrath, ordered us off and began laying up the rail fence, threatening all the while to go and get his gun and shoot us. Tom coolly laid his hand on the handle of his pistol, when the fellow suddenly changed his mind and went home and we left him to nurse his wrath and lay up his fence, which otherwise we would have put up as we found it. His object, it seems, was to compel us to stay over night at his place, and buy grain of him.

Monday, April 12, 1852. Tonight we pitch our camp for the first time. Our campground is a beautiful little prairie, covered with grass and we feel quite at home and very independent.

Tuesday, April 13th. Soon after we struck the Des Moines River and traveled up the north bank, passing through Ottumwa, the prettiest place we have yet seen and have decided to come here and make our home when we return from California with a fortune. Camped this evening on the bank of a little stream. While we were eating supper a lady who lives close by came to see, as she said, how campers did.

Sunday, May 16th. While we were getting supper, the Pawnee chief and twelve of his braves came and expressed a desire to camp with us. Their appetites are very good and it takes quite an amount of provisions to entertain them hospitably, but some willow boughs strewn around the camp fire suffices them for a bed.

Sunday, May 30th. There is a very large camp here and most of them are remaining for the day. There was preaching this afternoon and it seems more like Sunday than any since we left home.

Tuesday, June 15th. About three o'clock we came opposite Fort Laramie. Some of the boys went over to the fort to mail letters. There are two or three nice looking houses in the fort, the first we have seen since leaving the Missouri River.

Sunday, July 4th. It has been so windy and dusty today that some times we could scarcely see the length of the team, and it blows so tonight that we cannot set the tent or get any supper, so we take a cold bite and go to bed in the wagons. The wagons are anchored by driving stakes in the ground and fastening the wagon wheels to them with ox chains.

Sunday, July 25th. This is the most like Sunday of any day since we left home, and we feel very much at home here.

Monday, July 26th. Wash day.

Tuesday, July 27th. Ironing and baking today.

Saturday, September 18th, 1852. We started down the valley, passing a house on the way, which I must describe as it is the first California house we have seen. It is three logs high, about six feet long, and four wide, one tier or clapboard or shakes as they are called here, covering each side of the roof. Leaving this, and passing through a gate we soon came to another cabin of larger dimensions.

Sunday, September 19th. About noon we arrived at Father's cabin, where we consider our journey ended, after traveling almost constantly for more than five months. Several called to pay their respects to "father Mac" as he is affectionately called by the miners, and to get a glimpse of his two daughters, a woman being a rare sight here. One enthusiastic miner declared he would give an ounce of gold dust for the sight of a woman's sunbonnet."

MEMOIRS OF TRAVEL, 1852

Newton G. Finley, 1922

> *Written some seventy years after the writer's cross-country emigration, this detailed description of his trip west is written with the exuberance that many pioneers felt as they journeyed to their new homes.*

The first week of April, 1852, the families mentioned below started from my Father's home in Saline County, Missouri, for San Jose, California.

Benjamin Campbell and wife, Mary Louisa Campbell
James Washington Finley and wife, Margaret Jane Finley
Their children
William Asa Finley
Newton Gleaves Finley
Sarah Esther Finley
John Pettis Finley
Hugh McNary Finley
Ann Eliza Finley
James Benjamin Finley

Ira Joseph Lovell and wife, Ann Laurette Lovell
Their Children
William McNary Lovell

James Michael Lovell
Mary Elizabeth Lovell
John Alexander Lovell
Theodore Campbell Lovell
Joseph Worth Lovell
Hugh McNary Lovell
Sarah Margaret Lovell

William Thornton Rucker and wife, Veranda Rucker
Their Children
Joseph E. Rucker
John S. Rucker
William Dodds Rucker
Robert Thornton Rucker
Hiram Newton Rucker
Zachariah Taylor Rucker
George Furgesson Rucker
Nancy Catherine Rucker

Robert Campbell and wife, Mary Ann Campbell
Their Children
David Campbell
John Campbell
Laura Campbell
Virginia Campbell

Teamster for W. T. Rucker - Steve Haskell
Teamster for B. Campbell - Jack Renison
Teamster for I. J. Lovell - John Wood
Teamster for J. W. Finley - Tom Midsinger

Teamster for J. W. Finley - Slack Plein
Assistant Cook for J. W. Finley - Black Sam
Assistant Cook for B. Campbell - James Slater
(Whole number of souls, Forty-four)
(Of which number only eight are known to be alive)

Tents and Supplies

Each family prepared tents for themselves and also looked after their own supplies of food. These tents were of simple durable construction; the frame consisting of three poles of convenient proportions; two being of the same length used as uprights, the third used as a ridge-prier and indicating the length of tent. These three timbers being then ingeniously united, completed the framework then with the cloth covering and ropes for anchoring with the necessary stakes for pinning in the earth, and the sleeping quarters are complete. Cooking vessels consisted of pots with bails or handles attached, and large Dutch Ovens for baking bread. The arrangements for hanging vessels over the fire were made by taking two iron rods of equal length pointed at one end with rings formed at the opposite extremity, sufficiently large to admit a good stout steel bar and hooks, then we have the outfit complete for boiling food and preparing all liquid refreshments. Fuel was a big factor, and on the open plains consisting largely of buffalo chips and sage brush. Water was abundant and of good quality. Our supply of food was bountiful and of the best grade also of great variety, consisting in part of: cornmeal, flour, buckwheat flour, ham, bacon, sausages, dried beef, beans, peas, potatoes, rice, coffee, tea, sugar, honey, syrup, milk, butter, dried fruits, apples (green), walnuts, hickory nuts, hazel nuts, etc. Each family did their own cooking. We had fresh milk twice daily, butter fresh daily, procured simply by placing milk at morning in the churn, put it aboard the wagon, at night we had the genuine article.

At this time will be given the name of the individual person who so successfully piloted this noble band of pioneers in the far distant "Golden West." This man was experienced, tried and true, a man that had passed over the same trail in the year 1846, and hence had a personal knowledge of all the conditions; a man to whom fear was unknown, a man among men; modest and retiring, one of God's nobler men, a man that dared to do and to be; a man that stood Four Square. His name, known to all pioneers of the Pacific Coast, is none other than Benjamin Campbell. Requiescat in Pace.

Our conveyances consisted of covered wagons known as Prairie Schooners, to the number of eight, with the addition of two family carriages; the wagons were drawn by oxen, the carriages were moved by mule power.

The livestock of the entire company brought over were made up of oxen and loose cattle, mostly cows; number some three hundred head; also about twenty mules and a few choice saddle horses.

The first day we traveled eight miles and camped at the home of my Grandfather Finley, near Marshall, the County Seat. Next morning at nine A.M. we pulled out for Lexington, and in due time we landed at Independance, our last camping ground prior to entering the great Indian Territory. At our first night's resting camp, after leaving the Missouri state boundary line, we encountered a very severe wind and rain storm. During the night our horses and cattle had a general stampede, causing more or less confusion, and succeeded in damaging one mule to the extent of badly fracturing a front leg, thus rendering him useless for the trip. So a trade was made with a band of Sioux Indians; we received in exchange a large red silk handkerchief, while they became the owner of the unfortunate mule.

Early the next morning the train was in moving order, ready to meet any emergency that came our way. The first streams of water engaging our attention were the Little and Big Blue Rivers: beautiful small streams of most clear blue looking water with pebbly bottoms, shaded with lovely foliage on all sides, located in such a charming open country, and last but not least the richness of the soil was the climax. We had the pleasure and satisfaction of spending two nights in this magnificent country. The next body of water on our journey was the South Fork of the Platte River; a tributary of the Missouri. We traveled for a number of days along near this stream; finally crossing to the northern side This river at first view presents a very novel appearance, located in a flat, open country; the flow of water is very quiet, of a muddy color, extremely shallow, not more than twenty inches in depth, with low sandy banks and unprotected by trees or shrubbery of any kind, the width of this stream is not less than one-half to three quarters of a mile. Lest it be forgotten in this locality we came up with the Patterson brothers of Missouri with a band of thirty thousand sheep destined for the Pacific Coast; a novel sight to behold, these inoffensive thrifty animals moving steadily onward as if propelled by some magic hand.

In a few days travel we arrived at the North Platte, a river of good depth, but comparatively narrow at this point. The wagons, we crossed over by means of a Toll bridge, the cattle, horses and mules we had to swim over which was accompanied with some risk to life, also such valuable time and patience were called into requisition. To make this proposition intelligible, will say there was good sized low island near the middle of the river; to this point the animals went very readily; when it came to urging them to take the water for the opposite shore, then the trouble and confusion began; for some time it seemed all our efforts were unavailing to accomplish our design. Finally our captain of the train suddenly got wise Selecting six expert horsemen, seated on good mounts, all trained for such an emergency, ropes were placed around the heads of the rebellious leaders, then horse and rider boldly and definitely plunged into the stream

leading in tow these incorrigible bovines soon to land them on the opposite shore. A few object lessons of this kind, then the remaining herd took
to the water and were again united with those that were piloted over so
unceremoniously. Fort Larimer then a Government Military Station is
located on the North side of this river. Near this fort we camped for the
night. This was a most beautiful broad expanse of country, the air is so
pure and hence distant objects could be discerned so very clearly, and at
the same time appeared to be so near. This land is very fertile, produces
abundant feed for stock and in the days of the early Pioneers to the West
was the banner range for the immense herds of Buffalo which at that time
ranged freely over these vast plains. "Monarch of all he surveyed."

In 1853 all is changed. Only one of these animals (once so numerous) was seen by our company and he showed up to poor advantage; coming from the North at full speed, he passed directly through the-train of
wagons, disappeared in a southerly direction, and making his escape from
his pursuers by plunging head-long into the North Platte River and succeeded in gaining the opposite shore. We were now in an Indian country,
yet we had no trouble with these people, as we were very cautious, keeping guards out at night around the cattle; the horses and mules at night
were regularly brought to the camp and enclosed in a circle, which was
formed by the wagons being placed at regular distances apart and then
connected by means of coupling chains.

The tents were set up outside this circle, in close proximity to the
wagons; and thus we managed every night while in this primitive country
exposed as we were constantly to the ravages of these bands of roving savage Indians.

Here will be told recollections of a picture formed on memory's
tablet concerning a place we passed on our trip; a beautiful picture never
to be effaced. A veritable City of Stone: Cliffs of rock standing out on the
open plain arrayed in majestic grandeur lifting their beautiful symmetrical

spires heavenward, proclaiming to all beholders, "The hand that made us is Divine."

Next commences a little drama. At midnight while the heavens were most gorgeously illuminated with the millions of brilliant twinkling stars, when all seemed so peaceful and quiet, "Natures sweet restorer, balmy sleep" was giving rest and comfort to the weary and tired ones; suddenly the cry of an infant babe is wafted on the slumbering denizens of the camp, and lo, we have with us a most welcome visitor: a beautiful, bright, sweet little girl baby Sarah Margaret. One day's delay; rest and congratulations, then-the caravan is again on the advance.

Here will be noted a little scene that has been unintentionally overlooked. Early one morning as the train moved out for the day, attention was called to the home of the Prairie Dog, truly a city inhabited by these denizens of the earth. Innumerable mounds of soil of various heights and of good size; each mound or elevation presented a lifely scene, as the entire family, young and old were very conspicuously arranged as if for a free exhibition; mutely saying by their many manoeuvres, "We are this day on dress parade."

Now for the Rocky Mountains: They are located to our west, not far distant, near which we journeyed many days.

One day at a distance we observed a band of antelope feeding quietly. They appeared to be so near and looked so life-like. Three of our young nimrods proposed to have an antelope stew; consulting "Captain Ben." He very modestly informed them, their venture was not feasible as the game was fully ten miles distant, in an open plain and hence the chances were all against them; so the antelope stew went glimmering.

Just as the wagons moved out for the day, one of our adventurous young men concluded it was a good opportunity to exhibit his skillfulness in handling his mount, a magnificent mule. By some means he failed to remain in the saddle, coming suddenly and very unceremoniously in collision with terra firma, a much surprised youngster, while the freed mule made a dash for liberty, making a bee-line for the distant mountain range, going some five miles, then circling gradually around on the return, having made the circuit of fifteen miles or more, none the worse for his morning's exercise.

We were now gradually ascending the Rocky Mountain Range and passing through the Black Hill Section: A very peculiar formation of bare, unproductive soil; mounds of various elevations indicating that at some time this entire section of country had experienced very severe earthquakes. For many days we were anxiously and expectingly looking for the hour to arrive when we could say positively that the summit of the Rockies had been reached; the ascent had been so very gradual it seemed almost incredible when it was announced that we were actually passing down on the Western slope in the direction of the Green River Country. Finding a suitable spot for the camp we called a halt and put up for the night. Here we had a stampede of the livestock, causing quite a commotion for a short time and damaging our valuable Bell Cow to the extent of putting her out of commision.

Green River, a feeder of the Great Colorado next came to our view. A most beautiful stream of pure mountain water, situated in and watering a lovely commodious valley destined at some day to be the dwelling place of many a prosperous and happy family. As we approached the river we found to our astonishment a great many emigrants in waiting to be crossed over to the opposite shore. Finally our time came, we were taken across by the Ferry, only the wagons and carriages with their belongings were thus handled; the loose stock crossed over by each "paddling their own canoe", thereby we gained such valuable time and saved many dollars in hard cash.

Breaking camp near Green River next morning we steered our course due West, climbing the Wahsatch Mountain, crossing the summit in due time, winding our way leisurely to the inviting plateau below where we landed in the vicinity of Fort Hall and near Bear River. Here we came near having a fatal accident. In crossing a small ravine, a six year old boy was thrown from the wagon, falling directly in front of the back wheel, which passed over his body, immediately above the hips. Strange to say, he was not seriously injured and in a few days to all appearances showed no signs of injury from his hasty tumble.

Taking a southerly turn we found ourselves near the Great Salt Lake where we camped for the night. Next morning as the caravan moved out for the day, Humboldt Mountains loomed up to our view. After travelling for some time we crossed over the summit and soon arrived at the headwaters of the Humboldt River, where we drove stakes for a night's repose.

Next day and for many days following, we traveled parallel with this noted river, through its valley with its wonderful growth of vegetation, its fertile soil and its many wells of water (many of them mineral) of almost every degree of temperature. Here let me narrate a story of a German emigrant. At the hour of camping, seeing one of these wells of mineral water, he proceeded to test the same by drinking. Soon he was more than satisfied, making haste to the camp he exclaimed as if in great fear: "Drive on my son John, drive on, hell is not one mile from this place." After camping many nights in these novel and interesting sections of the "wild and wooly West" we finally arrived at the sinks of this remarkable river, disappearing as it does beneath the burning sands of the great thirty-five mile desert. We arrived at this locality in the afternoon; camped for the night, remained here until next day about three P.M.: giving the animals a good rest, time to feed up for the long drive and also to fill all available vessels with water for our comfort. At the designated hour, having taken every known precaution, we pulled out into this uninviting, sandy, alkali, barren waste, travelling continuously for nearly fifteen hours we arrived just at the break of day safe, sane and sound in the unpretentious little city of Rag Town.

Before proceeding on our journey will simply say this northerly trail was chosen for the very many advantages it furnished; superior grazing facilities was quite a factor; then the water supply was another important consideration, it being of better quality and in greater abundance also more widely distributed and, last but not least, fuel for burning was a big item and on this route we found a good supply and easily procured.

The successful journey of our company to this point was very largely due to this fact: "Safety was our motto" and no travel on Sunday unless it was actually necessary. Specific regulations for all camping arrangements were in full force, every man in his place, a certain line of work to perform and no shirking. Early hours to halt the train was strictly enforced; so the cattle and horses could have ample time in which to secure their regular rations. Promptness was the keynote and contributed very largely to our successful and harmonious journey of six months. The crowning feature of all—"God was with us."

This article was written entirely from memory after a lapse of seventy years, by request of a friend. While no doubt, there may be some minor geographical inaccuracies, yet as a whole this writing is substantially correct. Facts are given and not fiction.

We will now retract this entire trip, using a recent map of the United States to locate our line of travel in reference to the boundary lines of these six newly made western states.

Leaving Independence, Missouri, we enter the state of Kansas near Atchison; taking a westerly direction, we pass the city of Marysville, continuing the same course we cross the Nebraska boundary line, pass near Fort Kerny; keeping the same general direction we come to the South Platte River; turning slightly to the west, we clip a corner off of Colorado; turning gradually northerly, we cross over the South Platte, invade Wyoming not far from Cheyenne; pursuing the same direction; cross the North Platte River at Fort Laramie; switching around through the Black Hills we cross Sweet Water (a small stream) scale the Rocky Mountain summit at South Pass; going due west we come to a Ferry near Green River. Now we are up against the Wahsatch Mountains, soon the summit is reached and then down the grade we find ourselves in the State of Idaho; next we cross little Bear River near Fort Hall; (here Robert Campbell and family left us, taking the Oregon Trail) turning southerly we pay our respects to Utah, come in close proximity to the Great Salt Lake, swinging westward we hail the State of Nevada, cross over the Humboldt Range; came to the headwaters of the Humboldt River following same to the sinks, reach the big sandy alkali desert, cross over at night and at early dawn enter the City of Rag Town.

We are now in Rag Town. About the middle of September; time admonishes us (as the snowy season is approaching) to move forward and cross over the Sierras to the "Land of Sunshine, Raisin Trees and Olive Groves". So we clean house, casting away all old shoes, discarded hats and worn Out garments to further adorn and embellish this noted and picturesque little village. The word is given to get in moving trim, when a man is observed approaching the camp; he inquires for the Campbell encampment. To our great astonishment and surprise he proved to be a messenger bearing good news from California in the person of William Campbell, coming all the distance alone to welcome us to his adopted Home Land.

After very many congratulations and hand shakings the caravan gets in motion. We cross the Carson River, a beautiful small stream of pure cold mountain water located near the base of the "High Sierras." We had been informed of the difficulties to be encountered in ascending this noted and far-famed mountain chain; we found by experience the t'half had not been told." The road at first sight appeared to be utterly impassable, the trail was so very narrow and such a steep grade, and Oh! the roughness of this so-called much traveled highway. To all difficult under-takings there must be a finish; so with the "Ancient Worthy" we can truly say: "Veni, Vidi, Vici, We came, we saw, we conquered."

After the turmoil, vexation and difficulties of the memorable day, we find ourselves near Truckee Lake, where we endeavor to secure a night's rest. Early the next morning when about ready to continue our journey, two bold mountaineers on horseback approach our captain, ask our des-tination, pass the compliments of the day, wish us a safe and prosperous journey, pass down the line of livestock, select as souvenirs our choice cow and a very valuable mule, switch them very hurriedly down a con-venient side trail, rush them into a deep narrow brushy ravine and away. All that could be said or done amounted to nothing—dies infaustus.

We continued our journey toward the summit and crossed over with-out any serious embarrassment. Scarcity of feed for the animals being our chief difficulty. Now for the descent into the beautiful verdant valleys, the Grand Canyons and gurgling streams awaiting our coming. In time we reached the once famed city of Hang Town (now Placerville) where we camped for the night. On a little stream of water near this place we youngsters were given milk pans and here we made our initial search for gold. Pulling up the grass with the roots attached, we filled our pans with water and by properly washing the contents we succeeded in obtaining quite a good showing of the precious metal.

Our next camping place was at Shingle Springs, some fifteen miles from Hang Town. We found here excellent grazing for our cattle and mov-ing by easy stages, gradually coming to the settlements. Finally we arrived in the City of Stockton at that time a small unpretentious town of a few hundred inhabitants. Here we tarried for one night. Next morning early, we broke camp and were on our way for the San Joaquin River where we arrived in good trim and crossed over the same without any difficulty.

After resting over from our day's travel, next morning we were again on the road and in a short time we entered Livermore Valley, camped at a small place by that name. The next day we passed out aver the hills to the west and through a charming little valley surrounded on all sides by such enchanting views. Amidst these imposing surroundings we were ushered into the beautiful Santa Clara Valley. We camped for the night near the San Jose Mission, just out in the valley west of the Warm Springs.

Next morning found us early on our journey; we made good time and very soon crossed over the Coyote Creek about noon, and ere long we entered "the Pueblo de San Jose" to our great delight and satisfaction. Continuing on in a westerly direction for three miles we arrived on the Gravel Ridge, near the now "noted Winchester residence" where our long and interesting journey ends—October 1, 1852.

<blockquote>
Many things more remain untold
Of this trip to the land of Gold
By the way—sufficient to say
We landed safe in San Jose.
</blockquote>

A LETTER FROM MARTHA S. READ
TO LORINDA SHELTON

Norwich, Chenago Co., New York, April 16, 1852

> *Women were often reluctant travelers on the Oregon Trail, as this letter from Martha Read to her sister shows. At a time when married women couldn't vote or own property (in most states) and career women were almost unheard of, the husband's decision was often the family's decision.*

Beloved sister I have seated myself for the purpose of writing a few lines to you to inform you that we are all well as usual excepting I am pretty much tired out a fixing for California we expect to start next monday which will be the 19 there is a great many a going from these parts and a great many families that we are acquainted with the roads are quite bad here now we have had a very backward spring but we think it will do to start by monday we are a going with two waggons one span of horses three yoke of cattle two cows we take a tent with us and a small stove and things for our comfort as far as we can but be assured it looks like a great undertaking to me but Clifton was bound to go and I thought I would go rather than stay here alone with the children I spoke about going there to stay with you but Clifton thought it want best he thought we had better all hang together and then we should not be a worrying about each

93

other I hope to live to see the day to come back and live among you but life is uncertain I have one thing to comfort me I know that I have the same God to protect me a going to California that I have here.

INTERESTING STORY OF HIS EXPERIENCE IN HUNTING BUFFALO COMING ACROSS THE PLAINS

James Longmire, Tacoma Sunday Ledger, *1892*

> *In 1853, when James Longmire crossed the Great Plains on his way to a new home in Washington, buffalo—or bison— numbered in the tens of thousands in herds that stretched throughout the western landscape. By the time he wrote this piece for the* Tacoma Sunday Ledger, *bison were all but extinct in the American West. Western emigration had taken its toll on the shaggy beasts and on the native cultures that depended on them for survival.*

As I am one of the pioneers of Washington, in her territorial days, I will fall in line with the many who have already written, and attempt a description of our trip across the plains, and subsequent events. It may not be out of place to remind the newcomers of today that they have little cause for complaint of hardships and suffering as compared with those who made that long tiresome journey thirty-nine and more years ago.

Through unbroken forests, over swollen streams, unknown and dangerous, over the dessert with its scorching sun and blistering sands, exposed to warlike and hostile Indians, disease, and many other perils which you will doubtless perceive before the close of my narrative. I started from our home in Shuwme Prairie, Fountain County, Indiana, on the 6th of March 1853, with my wife and four children, Elcaine, David, John and Tibatha. John, the youngest, was not able to walk when we started, but learned his first steps with the help of the tongue of our ox wagon while crossing the plains, holding to it for support, and walking from end to end while in camp evenings.

John B. Moyer, a very finished young man who had studied for the ministry, but who was at that time teaching our district school, went with us; also Joseph Day, a son of our neighbors. I got a neighbor to drive us to Athicia, the nearest town, where we took passage on the U.S. Aiel, a little streamer running on the Wabash River. Evansville at that time was a flourishing town of 4,000 or 5,000 inhabitants.

A shocking incident of our first start was the bursting of the boiler of the steamer Bee, twelve miles from Evansville, which caused the death of every person aboard. The U.S. Aiel took the poor mangled creatures aboard and carried them to Evansville, where they were met by grief-stricken, who had sighted the signal of morning displayed by our steamer.

From Evansville, we took the streamer Sparrow Hawk for St. Louis, thence by the Polar Star up the Mississippi River to St. Joseph. We were now upward of 2,000 miles on our westward journey. There I bought eight yoke of oxen and a large quantity of supplies and proceeded in wagons along the river to Cainsville, now Council Bluffs, and camped. As it was yet too early to start on our long journey, the grass not grown sufficient to feed our oxen along the routes we decided to remain for several weeks and make some preparations for another start. I bought a carriage and span of horses for $250, which Mrs. Longmire and the children were to use as far as the road would permit. I also got a sheet-iron stove, which with utensils for cooking, only weighed twenty-five pounds, but which proved a real luxury, as we were thus able to have warm biscuits for breakfast whenever we chose, besides many other delicacies which we could not have by camp fires. For the stove, I paid $12, though to us it proved almost invaluable. At Cainsville, I stood guard at night for the first time in my life, in company with Van Ogle, who was also camped here, preparatory to going to Puget Sound. It was dark one evening when I finished the feeding of my cattle, so I could not see the person who spoke in a fine, childish voice, saying, "Is there a man here by the name of Longmire?" I thought it must be a boy, judging by his voice, and told him that was my name, whereupon he introduced himself as John Lane. A man of whom I had often heard, but never had seen a tall man, well-built, with a smooth, boyish face, and fine squeaking voice, much out of keeping with his great body. He invited me to his camp nearby, where I met his brother-in-law, Arthur Sargent, and his family. After some conversation, we made arrangements to continue our journey together. While here, we met a young man by the name of Iven Watt, who was anxious to cross the plains. I engaged him to drive one of my ox teams, and found him an excellent help at various times when obstacles met us which seemed hard to overcome. His friend, William Claflin, hired to Mr. Sargent to assist his son and Van Ogle with Sargent's ox team.

The time had now come when we decided that there was grass for the cattle on the way and we moved twelve miles below Council Bluffs to a ferry, where we crossed the Missouri river, making our final start fir Puget Sound on the 10th of May, 1853. We camped for the night about one mile from the ferry, where we were joined by E. A. Light, now of Steilacoom, a friend of John Lane's. Nothing occurred worthy of note until two days afterward when we reached the Elk Horn river, where we found a ferry with only one boat, and so many emigrants ahead of us that we must wait for two or three weeks to be ferried over. A party of emigrants was lucky enough to get three canoes, and while they were crossing we all went to work and made one more. By this time they were across, so we bought their canoes, and with our own proceeded to ferry our goods over the river. Here occurred an accident, which proved disastrous, and spoiled, in a measure, the harmony existing in our little company of emigrants.

John Lane had started with some fine stock, among which was a thoroughbred mare of great beauty and very valuable, which he would not allow to swim with the rest of our stock safely across the stream. But with a rope around her neck, held by Sargent and myself on one side the river and by himself and E. A. Light on the other side, would tow her across, which we did, but alas, dead. We landed the beautiful creature, after following Lane's instructions, and tried to revive her, but she was dead. Poor Sargent had to bear the blame, unjustly I think, and only escaped blows from Lane, whose rage knew no bounds, by my interference. But he left our party after begging me to go with him, and in company with E. A. light, Samuel and William Ray, and a man named Mitchell continued his journey. We regretted the loss of his beautiful mare and the unpleasantness between him and Sargent, which caused him to leave our party, for friends were few and far from home, consequently much dearer. But these friends we were to meet again, which we little expected when we parted. Two hundred miles further on we came to Rawhide creek, a pretty stream with its banks bordered by graceful waving willows, cool and green.

This was the last tree or shrub we were destined to see for 200 miles. Here we stopped to rest our now thoroughly tired, foot-sore oxen, and do our washing, which was not done always on Monday, much to the annoyance of our excellent housekeepers who, at home, had been accustomed to thus honoring blue Monday. We had killed a few antelope along the road, which furnished our camp with what we thought the best steak we had ever eaten, and were fired with a resolve to secure a still greater luxury, in which we had not yet indulged. We had seen several small bands of buffalo, but with no opportunity of capturing any of them. So I selected Iven Watt, a crack shot, by the way, as my companion, and with our rifles on our shoulders, mounted my carriage horses, and with bright hopes and spirits high, started out to bring in some buffalo meat and thus further prove our skill as hunters from the Hoosier state. We left Mayer and Day to guard the camp, assist the women with the washing, and kill jackrabbits, game too small for us. We rode about fifteen miles to the north, when we came upon two buffaloes quietly feeding upon a little slope of ground. We dismounted, picketed our horses, and on all fours crept toward them till barely within range of our muzzle-loading rifles, when they saw us. We fired without hitting either of them, and they started toward us. We ran for our horses, which we luckily reached and lost no time in mounting, when the buffalo turned and ran from us across the level plain. Going on a little further we came to a ridge, or elevation, which afforded protection for our horses, which we once more picketed, and walking about a hundred yards came upon a herd of the coveted game, from which we selected a large bull, and commenced firing upon him. We fired nine shots apiece, but still our game did not fall. He would snort loudly, and whirl round as if dazed, not knowing from whence came the bullets, and not seeing us from our hiding place in the ridge of ground. Seeing our shots did not bring our game, I told Watts we were firing too high, and reloading we took aim and fired at the same time, but lower and with effect. To our great joy the huge creature fell. Rushing back to our horses we mounted and hurried to secure our prize, which lay on the ground only wounded. Upon seeing us, he staggered to his feet and ran about a hundred yards, when he fell again. The rest of the herd, frightened at our approach, ran wildly across the plain with uplifted tails, and were soon out of sight. Seeing our buffalo could not run, I sprang from my horse, and taking fair aim at his head, fired and killed him, contrary to a theory I had heard that a buffalo could not be killed by a shot in the head. Again we secured our horses, and began to strip our game of his smooth coat, taking the hindquarters for our share, judging this to be the choicest cut, which we were to put in a bag which we carried for the purpose.

Little we know of life and customs on the plains. In about fifteen minutes after we began our work we were surprised—yes, perfectly horror-stricken—to see about thirty big, hungry gray wolves coming rapidly towards us, attracted by the scent of blood from the dead buffalo. Nearer and nearer they came, till hearing a noise we looked toward our horses, only to see them running in the wildest affright, on, on to the north, in a directly opposite course from camp. We left our game to the wolves willingly, having no wish to contest their claim to it, and went in pursuit of our horses. We had intended to be in camp with our buffalo meat in time for dinner, and had set out in the morning without a morsel of food in our pockets. So nightfall found us hungry, tired, afoot, and miles—how many we knew not—from camp and friends, our horses gone and hardly knowing which way to turn. However, it was a starlight night, and fixing my eye on one bright star, I said to Watt that we must take that star for our guide and go as far as we could that night. We went on, Watt complaining of hunger very often, until the sky became cloudy and we could no longer see our guide, when we sat down and placed our guns on the ground pointing toward the star that had been to us, so far, a welcome guide. The time we could not tell, as neither of us carried a watch, but it must have been far in the night.

From the time of leaving camp, the many mishaps of the day and our extreme fatigue, it seemed an age. Soon all trouble was forgotten in deep sleep, from which we awoke to find the sky clear and our late guide ready to light us on our weary journey. We arose and started once more, neither stopping for an instant or turning aside for rock, hill or bramble, but kept as nearly as possible in a straight line, never forgetting our star till it grew dim before the coming daylight. Thus we went, still fasting, over a beautiful rolling country, till about 9 or 10 o'clock in the morning, when we climbed a steep bluff and below us saw the Platte river valley through which slowly passed a few straggling emigrant wagons. The very sight of them brought joy to our hearts, and also relief to Watt's empty stomach, for the first thing he did on reaching the wagon was to ask for food, which was freely given. I inquired the way to Rawhide creek, which the emigrants had left two miles behind them. Being so near our own camp I did not ask for food, but Watt insisted on sharing his portion with me, which I accepted, and must say relished after my long fast. We hurried back to the camp, where I found my wife almost frantic with grief at our long absence, thinking of course, we had been killed by hostile Indians. Our friend Sargent was intending to continue his journey the next day if we did not return, but my wife was thinking of some plan by which she could return to our old home on the banks of the Wabash.

However, when we told them of our narrow escape, even with the loss of our horses and game, grief turned to joy, and peace reigned once more in our camp. After resting the remainder of the day we prepared, the next morning, not for a buffalo hunt but for a hunt for our lost horses. Mr. Sargent loaned us two of his horses, which we rode, and in case we did not return that evening he was to put two of his other horses to my carriage and proceed with Mayer, Day, my family and goods the next morning. We were to overtake them somewhere along the line. After making this arrangement we went back to the scene of our late adventure, where we found large herds of wild horses but never a track of our own, which, being shod, were easily tracked. We hunted till sundown when we came to a mound or hill, perhaps 100 or 150 feet above the level, with a circular depression or basin on the top of it, which we selected for our camp. Taking our horses into this basin we made them secure by hobbling them, took our supper, consisting of a cold lunch minus drink of·any kind. We witnessed from our elevated position a grand buffalo show—fully 5,000 scatted over that vast plain, many of them quite near the mound on which we stood. It seemed almost as far as we could see to be one vast herd of buffalo. We arose next morning and continued our hunt till the middle of the afternoon, when we gave up all hope of finding the lost horses, and taking a westerly course set out to overtake the wagons, which had stopped before night for our benefit. A buffalo hunt proved a source of joy as well as sorrow to our party for soon after camping for the night, Mayer saw two men, buffalo hunters, who, like Watt and myself, had been lost, riding our lost horses leisurely along the road. Going to them Mayer told them that the horses belonged in our camp. They said they had seen the horses on the plains, and knowing they had escaped from some emigrant train, caught them and gladly rode them into camp. They declined the $5 reward my wife and Mayer pressed upon them for the great service rendered. The previous day my wife and children had ridden in the ox wagon leaving our carriage to Mrs. Sargent and family in part payment for the borrowed horses. But the next day on resuming our journey she gladly gave up the cushions and comforts of the ox wagon for those of the carriage, which was once more drawn by the lost horses. Nothing further happened except the occasional killing of an antelope or stray buffalo, my desire for buffalo hunting not being fully satisfied, although I had vowed after my late adventure never to hunt buffalo again. Sargent and I killed one about this time, which weighed fully 2,500 pounds, whose meat was so tough we could not use it. He was evidently the patriarch of a large herd.

We crossed the Rocky Mountains at South Pass, according to instructions given in Horn's guidebook for emigrants, which we had carefully observed during our trip. It gave minute instructions as to proper camps, roads, the crossing of streams, where to find good water and grass, and other information which we found of great value, as our experience afterward proved. Some days after crossing the mountains our party was increased by the families of Tyrus Himes, father of George Himes of Portland, Oregon, and Judson Himes of Elma, and Mr. Dodge, who settled, on their arrival here, on Mima prairie. All went smoothly till we crossed Bear River mountains, and, feeling some confidence in our camp judgment, we had grown somewhat careless about consulting our guide book, often selecting our camp without reference to it. One of these camps we had good cause to remember. I had gone ahead to find a camp for noon, which was on a pretty stream with abundance of grass for our horses and cattle, which greatly surprised us, as grass had been a scarce article in many of our camps. Soon after dinner, we noticed some of our cattle beginning to lag and seem tired and some of them began to vomit. We realized with horror that our cattle were poisoned, so we camped at the first stream we came to, which was Ham's fork of Bear river, to cure if possible our poor sick cattle. Here we were eighty or a hundred miles from Salt Lake, the nearest settlement, in such a dilemma. We looked about for relief. Bacon and grease were the only antidotes for poison, which our stores contained. We cut bacon in slices and forced a few slices down the throats of the sick oxen, but after once tasting it the poor creatures ate it eagerly, thereby saving their lives, as those that did not eat it (cows we could spare better than our oxen) died next day. The horses were none of them sick. Had we consulted our guide before, instead of after camping at the pretty spot, we would have been spared all this trouble, as it warned travelers of the poison existing there. This event run our stock of bacon so low we were obliged to buy more, for which we paid 75 cents per pound, and 50 cents per pound for butter, which we bought of Mr. Melville, one of our party.

We were joined at Salmon falls by a Mr. Hutchinson and family. Here we crossed Snake River the first time, a quarter of a mile above the falls. Hutchinson had a fine lot of horses and cattle, which caused him much anxiety, as he was afraid they would drown while crossing the river. There were a great many Indians here of the Snake tribe, and he tried to hire one of them to swim his stock, offering him money, which he stubbornly refused to do. Finally Hutchinson took off his overshirt, a calico garment, and offered it to him. This was the coveted prize. He took it, swam four horses safely, drowned one, then when he reached the opposite side quietly mounted one of the best horses and rode rapidly away over the hills, leaving us to the difficult task of crossing, which we did without further accident. We paid $4 for every wagon towed across the river. For 200 miles, we wended our weary way, on to Fort Boise, a Hudson Bay trading post, kept by an Englishman and his Indian wife, the former being the only white person at the post. Here we had to cross Snake River again, which at this point was a quarter of a mile wide. The agent kept a ferry and would not take our wagons over for less than $8 apiece, which was as much again as we had been paying at other crossings. I tried to get an Indian to swim our cattle over, but failing, Watt proposed to go with them if I would, which seemed a fair proposition, and as they would not go without someone to drive them, we started across. Watt carried a long stick in one hand, holding by the other to the tail of old Lube, a great rawboned ox who had done faithful service on our long, toilsome journey. I threw my stick away and went in a little below Watt, but found the current very strong, which drifted me down stream. I thought I should be drowned and shouted to Watt, "I'm gone." With great presence of mind he reached his stick toward me, which I grasped with a last hope of saving my life, and by this means bore up till I swam to Watt, who caught on the tail of the nearest ox. Thus giving me a welcome hold on old Lube's tail, who carried me safely to the shore. Only for Watt's coolness and bravery, I should have lost my life at the same spot where one of Mr. Melville's men was drowned on the previous evening.

At Grande Ronde, a happy surprise awaited us. Nelson Sargent, whose father was in our party, met John Lane, who arrived in advance of us, with the welcome news that a party of workmen had started out from Olympia and Steilacoom to make a road for us through the Natchez pass over the Cascade Mountains. Ours being the first party of emigrant to attempt a crossing north of The Dalles, on the Columbia River. Lane waited at Grande Ronde while Nelson Sargent pushed ahead to meet his aged parents. Our party was reunited at Grande Ronde. E. A. Light, John Lane and others, who had left us at the Elkhorn River, met us and continued the journey with us across the Cascade Mountains. We went fifty miles further to the Umatilla River, where we rested two days and made preparations for the rest of our trip. Lest our provisions run short, I bought, at a trading post here, 100 pounds of flour, for which I paid $40 in gold coin, unbolted flour too.

We left the emigrant trail at Umatilla and with thirty-one wagons struck out for Fort Walla Walla now Wallula. Fifty miles further on was a trading post kept by an agent of the Hudson Bay company. Of him we bought lumber—driftwood from the Columbia river—of which we made a flatboat on which to tow our goods across, afterward selling it, or trading its to the agent in payment for the lumber. On the 8th of September, at 2 o'clock in the afternoon, our boat was finished, and the task of crossing commenced. It was not a pleasant task, but by working all night, everything was safely launched by sunrise next morning except our cattle and horses. These we wanted the Indians to take across for us. Sargent was the only man who could speak Chinook, but not well enough to make a bargain with the Indians, so we got the agent to hire them to swim our stock. Before they would commence the work, they must be paid. We gave them $18, and they brought up twenty-five canoes, formed in line below the crossing, and we drove our cattle in the stream, and they swam to shore safely. Next came the horses. When they were about the middle of the river the treacherous Indians laid down their oars and made signs, which I understood to mean more money. Meanwhile our horses were drifting down stream, where high bluffs rose on either side, and they could not possibly land. Taking out my purse, I offered them more money and they at once took up the oars and paddled across, landing our horses safely. The chief of the Walla Wallas was Pupi Pupu Muxmux, or Yellow Serpent, a very important person who rode, with the dignity of a king, a large American horse, a beautiful bay, with holsters on his saddle, and a pair of navy revolvers. He was a large, fine looking Indian, fully aware of his power as a chief, which was well demonstrated when we divided among our party some beef we had bought of him. It was cut in pieces varying from ten to twenty pounds, but it must be weighed. The chief 'Went to Mr. Melville, the only man in our party who had scales for weighing, and taking them in his hand examined them closely, although he could not tell one figure from another. Then, looking carefully at the many faces around him, seeming satisfied with the scrutiny, he came to me, gave me the scales with a sign that I do the weighing, at the same time seating himself flat on the ground amongst us. I weighed, Lane standing by with book and pencil to tally. Every time a piece was weighed Pupi Pupu Muxmux would spring up, examined the scales closely, give a grunt which meant yes, and sit down; and so on until the last piece was weighed, Lane making settlement with him for our party. Pupi Pupu Muxmux was killed at the battle of Walla Walla during a four-day engagement in the spring of 1856 while trying to make his escape from the volunteers. Who held him as a friendly Indian, to join his tribe, which he had represented as friendly, but who were really waging bitter warfare against the white settlers. A brother of this chief was hired to guide us to the Natchez pass.

I must not forget to tell you that at Walla Walla we saw the home of the noble Marcus Whitman. A log house covered with straw held on by poles laid across the roof. A little garden and orchard were enclosed near the house, and a little further on we saw the graves of Whitman, his wife, and heroic little band who were massacred by the Indians some time before our arrival.

Our guide made a horse trade with Mr. Melville, in which he considered himself cheated, grew indignant and deserted us, and we were left in that strange country without a landmark, a compass, or guide nothing to help us. We traveled on, however, to the Yakima River, which we crossed, and here lost by death one of our party, Mrs. McCullough, a relative of Mrs. Woolery, now one of Puyallup's esteemed citizens. Until this sad event, she was the life, the sunshine of our party. Everyone loved "Aunt Pop," as she was familiarly called, but the death of her friend cast a shadow over her bright face, and made the remainder of our journey gloomy when we thought of the lonely grave by the Yakima. Our next obstacle was a canyon at Well Springs, which seemed impossible to cross. From the Yakima River we had been followed by a band of Indians, who had kept our wives and children in perfect terror, but laughed and chatted gaily as they rode along. The tyees or big men were dressed in buckskin leggings, handsomely beaded, and breech-clouts, made of cedar bark. The squaws were dressed very similarly. Men and squaws all had painted faces. The squaws always carried the papooses done up in proper Indian fashion and hung to the horn of the saddle, which bobbed up and down in no very easy manner when the ponies were in full gallop. At Well Springs, we sent out men to find a better road, as we thought we were lost. The Indians, knowing from this move that we were lost got off their ponies, cleared a small piece of ground and marked two roads, one heading northeast, the other northwest, making dots at intervals along each road, the former having fewer dots than the latter. One of them, motioning his head in an upward and curving line, pointed with the other hand to the dots, saying at each one, "sleeps, sleeps," and at the end of the road, "soldiers," the only words we could understand, and really all the English they could speak. Lane said to me: "What shall we do?" I replied, "Let us take the road which has the fewest 'sleeps,'" which we did, going northeast one or two days, when we knew we had taken the wrong road. We had no compass, and would have known but little more if we had had one. We saw before us almost a perpendicular bluff, seemingly 1,000 feet high, extending far away to the mountains. This we learned later was White Bluffs, on the Columbia River. Here we camped for the night, ordering the Indians to camp at a respectful distance from us, which they did. We placed a double guard out, as we suspected they had led us to this trap in order to massacre our whole party. I really believe now that their intentions were good, if they could have told us, so we could have understood them. The next day we retraced our way to Well Springs, where we had left our proper course. In due time we learned that our Indian escort meant to conduct us to Fort Colville, an English trading post, for the winter, thinking the snow on the Cascades would prevent our reaching Fort Steilacoom, where United States soldiers were stationed. Upon reaching Well Springs, our followers left us, much to our relief. We were further encouraged the same night by the return of Nelson Sargent, who with others had gone in advance to look out a good road, with the glad news that after crossing the canyon a good road lay before us. Further, that they had struck the trail which the Steilacoom and Olympia Company had blazed for the coming emigrants.

On the 18th of September, as well as I remember, we crossed the canyon, or rather traversed its length about a mile, which was the roughest traveling I ever saw, and came out on a beautiful plain. We traveled along Coal creek for two days when we came to Selah Valley on the upper Yakima, which we crossed. Taking our course along Wenas creek, about ten miles, when we came to a garden, now the farm owned by David Longmire, which was kept by Indians of whom we bought thirteen bushels of potatoes. The first vegetables we had had since leaving the Rocky mountains a real feast, though, boiled in their jackets, a bucketful making one meal for us.

Following Wenas creek to its source, we crossed over to the Natchez

River, which we followed for four days, crossing and recrossing fifty-two times. Then left it and started for the summit of the Cascade Mountains, north of Mount Tacoma, which we reached in three days, finding fine grass and good water. Here we stopped for two days, giving our tired oxen a good rest and plenty of food, which they badly needed, for the rest of our journey. Three miles further on we came to Summit Hill, where we spliced ropes and prepared for the steep descent, which we saw before us. One end of the rope was fastened to the axles of the wagon, the other thrown around a large tree and held by several men and thus, one at a time, the wagons were lowered gradually a distance of 300 yards. When the ropes were loosened, and the wagons drawn a quarter of a mile further with locked wheels, when we reached Greenwater. All the wagons were lowered safely but the one belonging to Mr. Lane, now a resident of Puyallup, which was crushed to pieces by the breaking of one of our ropes, causing him and his family to finish the trip on horseback. At Summit Hill my wife and Mrs. E. A. Light went ahead of the wagon with their children, taking a circuitous trail which brought them around to the train of wagons, for which we made a road as we went. As they walked along the narrow trail, my wife before, they were surprised to meet a white man, the first they had seen aside from those in our party, since leaving Walla Walla. It proved to be Andy Burge, who had been sent out from Fort Steilacoom with supplies for the roadmakers, who had already given up the job for want of food, which arrived too late for them, but in time for us, whose stores had grown alarmingly low. No less surprised was Burge at meeting two lone women in the wilderness, who greeted them with: "My God, women, where in the world did you come from?" A greeting rough, but friendly in its roughness to the two women who shrank against the trees and shrubbery to allow him and his pack animal to pass them in the trail, which was barely wide enough for one person. From them he learned of our whereabouts, and came to us, trying to persuade us to return to where there was grass and water for our stock, telling us we could not possibly make the trip over the country before us. Failing in this, he set to work and distributed his supplies amongst us, and returned to Fort Steilacoom, blazing trees as he went, and leaving notes tacked to them, giving us what encouragement he could, and preparing us, in a measure, for what was before us. For instance, "The road is a shade better;" a little further on "a shade worse," then again, "a shade better," and so on, until we were over the bad roads. We crossed Greenwater River sixteen times, and followed that stream until we came to White River, which we crossed six times. Then left it for a dreary pull over Wind Mountain, which was covered with heavy fir and cedar trees, but destitute of grass, with a few vine maples, on whose leaves our poor oxen and horses lived for seven days, not having a blade of grass during that time. I must not forget to mention the fact that in these dark days—seven of them—we and our half-starved cattle worked the road every day. We bridged large logs which lay before us, by cutting others and laying alongside, making a bridge wide enough for the oxen to draw our wagons across. Then all, except John Lane, E. A. Light and myself, left their wagons on account of their failing oxen, which they drove before them to Boise Creek prairie, where there was good grass. Lane, Light, and I arrived first; the rest soon followed with their cattle and horses. Four miles further we reached Porter's prairie, where Allan Porter, now of Hillburst, had taken a claim, but who was at that time in Olympia. We again crossed White River, making the seventh time, and pushed on to Connell's prairie, thence to the Puyallup River, to the present site of Van Ogle's hop farm. Little did Van think then that he would ever raise, bale, and sell hops on that piece of ground. We found the river low and filled with humpback salmon. We armed ourselves with various weapons, clubs, axes and whatever we could get and went fishing. Every man who could strike a blow got a fish, and such a feast we had not enjoyed since we had potatoes boiled in the jackets, but fish was far ahead of potatoes. John Mayer declared they were the best fish he had ever eaten. We had a royal feast. Some of our party was up all night cooking and eating fish. All relished them but Mrs. Longmire, who was feeling indisposed, but she fortunately got a delicacy—rare to her—a pheasant, which she bought from an Indian—her first purchase on Puget Sound.

The next day we moved on to Nisqually plains and camped at Clover creek, some 300 yards from the home of Mrs. Mahan, who, I believe, still lives there, and whose kindness the ladies of our party will never forget. On the 9th of October, the day after we camped at Clover creek, the men all went out to Fort Steilacoom to see Puget Sound, and during our absence Mrs. Mahan made a raid on our camp and took my wife, Mrs. E. A. Light, Mrs. Woolery and other ladies whose names I do not remember, to her home, where she had prepared a dinner which to these tired sisters, after their toilsome journey, was like a royal banquet. After months of camp life, to sit once more at a table presided over by a friend in this far-away land, where we thought to meet only strangers, was truly an event never to be forgotten, and one to which my wife often refers as a bright spot on memory's page.

Before proceeding with my narrative I must mention the fact that I arrived in this country with torn and ragged pants and coat, my cap battered, with only one boot, my other foot covered with an improvised moccasin made of a portion of a cow's hide which we had killed a few days before. In this garb I was to meet a party of well dressed gentlemen from Olympia, who had heard of us from Andy Burge, led by Mr. Hurd, who had come out to welcome the first party of emigrants direct from the East over the Cascade mountains north of The Dalles. My garb was a sample of those of the other men, and when we were together felt pretty well, all being in the same fashion; but when brought face to face with well dressed men we felt somewhat embarrassed. But our new friends were equal to the emergency and our embarrassment was soon dispelled by copious draughts of "good old bourbon," to which we did full justice, while answering questions amidst introductions and hearty handshaking. This was on the 8th day of October.

On the 10th of October Dr. Tolmie, chief factor of Hudson Bay Company, stationed at Fort Nisqually, paid us a visit, asked us numerous questions about our long journey and arrival treated us in a very friendly manner, but soon left, bidding us a polite farewell. In about three hours he returned with a man driving an ox cart, which was loaded with beef just killed and dressed which he presented to us, saying, "Distribute this to suit yourselves." Not understanding it to be a present we offered to pay him, which he firmly but politely refused, saying, "it is a present to you," and it was a present most welcome to us at that time, and for which we expressed heartfelt thank to the generous giver. Leaving our families in camp, E. A. Light, John Lane and I started out to look for homes. Having received due notice from the Hudson Bay company not to settle on any lands north of the Nisqually River we crossed the river and went to Yelm prairie, a beautiful spot. I thought as it lay before us covered with tall waving grass, a pretty stream bordered with shrubs and tall trees, flowing through it, and the majestic mountain standing guard over all, in its snowy coat, it was a scene fit for an artist. Herds of deer wandered at leisure through the tall grass. It was good enough for me and I bought a house from Martin Shelton, but bought no land, as it was unsurveyed as yet and returned for my family. Hill Harmon was in camp waiting for my return. He had a logging camp on the Sound and wanted to hire my boys, John Mooyer, Iven Watt and Will Claffin, (the last name had joined us at Fort Hall) who declined his terms, $85 per month, until they knew I could get along without them. Knowing the boys were needy, I told them to go, which they did, soon, getting an advance in salary to $100 per month. We started for our new home, my wife and children in one wagon drawn by three yoke of oxen, which she drove. I went ahead with another wagon and four yoke of oxen. Our carriage had long ago been left on Burnt river, also the harness which we saw afterward on a pair of mules driven past us on the emigrant trail. Arrived "at home" we found a large number of Indians camped near by. About thirty of them came in to see us the first night to examine things new to them, which they did, expressing their surprise by grunts and guttural sounds which were Greek to us. We found but three white families for neighbors, Mr. Braile, a bachelor, Mr. and Mrs. Levi Shelton and Mr. and Mrs. Hughes, the latter now a citizen of Steilacoom. The following winter I took a donation claim, a portion of the farm on which I have since resided.

CROSSING THE PLAINS IN 1853

Reminiscences of Martha Ann Tuttle McClain
From Iowa to Oregon, via the Applegate Trail, 1903

Martha Ann Tuttle McClain, her husband, and three children emigrated to Oregon via the Oregon and Applegate Trails in 1853. This reminiscence, commenced in 1903 and finished by Martha in 1905, recalls vividly the cross-country trip and the beginnings of her new life. The memoir focuses a great deal on relations with Native Americans and ends with the beginning of the Indian wars in Jackson County. Her words and sentiments reflect the biases of her time, but they don't diminish the value of her reflections on the past.

Columbus, Wash.
Dec. the 15
1903

I hope you will not expect verry much from one of my age, for i shal be 76 the 23rd of this present month if I live that long. But my own children and many friends have asked me so often to write I have made up my mind I will do the best I can, hoping you will over look the imperfections and take it in the spirit it is given.

yours verry truly
your mother
Martha Ann McClain

Martha's Narrative

Now to commence back as far as I know. Both of my grandfathers fell in the war of the Revolution. My grandfather on my Father's side was Nathan H. Tuttle of english descent, Borne in England, on my Mother's side german. His name was Edward Faircluff. My Father name was Nathan Tuttle for his own Father. My Mother's name was Rosanna FairCluff. My Father and Mother were married about the year 1820 in the state of North Carolina. They emigrated to verginia whin I was an infant. My Father was imployed as overseer on the plantation of Blacks for some years then moved to the beautiful state of Ohio where I was raised to wamanhood. My Mother died in the State of Ohio in the year of 1840. I then came with my married sister and Brother in law to Iowa. My Father came out to Iowa after I had been there a year. It so happened that my Father's farm and that of a neighbour joined. Of course there was a young man in the neighbor's family and a young girl in my father's. So like other your people we agreed to make one house do for both of us so in the year of 1846 on the 2nd of july we were married. Mr. William Jackson McClain to Miss Martha Ann Tuttle of Knoxville, Marian Co., Iowa. My Husband was a Kentuckian by birth. His Father's name was Philip McClain, his mother Rachel Jinkens by name.

Now I'm coming to the shady part. Crossing the Plains in the 50s in the winter of 53. There happened to be a company making up to try their luck in the faraway land of gold in California. As we happened to be down there on a Christmas visit my husband became enthused with the spirit of adventure. On coming to dinner at his father's he remarked that he had a notion to go with the rest of the boys and try his luck. His father remarked "if you do i'll give you a horse to start on." Well, next day we went home and in less than two months he had sold our farm and every thing else that we did not want to bring with us eaven my loom and was ready to start with the rest. The Father, true to promice, the day before we started he sent a nice large bey horse to my husband.

On the 18 day of April 1853 we took up our march, bidding adue to friends to face we knew not what. Many friends assembled on the big prarie west of Knoxville, Iowa to take a last farewell look as we moved away. My only brother a boy of 15 dropped back and waved his hand-kerchief in token of a last farewell. We travailed all day through mud almost hub deep as any one knows that has ever seen an April break up in the middle states.

That night we came to White usually a little stream but now bank full. Well, we had to lay over a few days. They managed by cutting down trees to make a bridge for the women and children to cross on also to carry most of the goods over on. But the oxen had to pull the wagons over and we all felt like we had gained a great victory, not knowing what to look for next. So it went on. After a time we arrived at Council Bluffs at the crossing of the Misouri River. You can only imagine the number of teams already there waiting to cross.

The River was verry high and the boat could not in safety be over-loaded, so we had to take it by turns like going to mill. Although the Boat was a large steam ferry we had to wait several days before our turn came. After a time we were over I say we for we felt like one family now that we had left civilation behind. We drove out a few miles and camped for the first night in the Indian territory. For a day or two nothing unusual hap-pened. But one afternoon we spied in the distance coming toward us the white Plumes of a band of warriors coming back from a battle with the Soux. They were all painted up in good shape. As I had never seen an Indian before I felt I could go no farther. I begged my Husband to turn back, but no, there was no cowardice in him while I was a natural coward. Well the old redskins each one looked into the front of our wagons, gave a big whoop, and away they went. We drove on to what was called Ash creek by our guide Book and formed a correll. This was done by placing the wagons in the shape of a horseshoe leaving the open side to be guarded by two men or more if necessary. That night after those Indians had passed us while we were all sleeping soundly without the least fear of an enemy nigh, our whole herd of cattle jumped to their feet as suddenly as ever a flock of Black Birds left the barnyard, and away they ran. This was done by Indians creeping up so as to get among the cattle then sudenly jumping up, giving their blankets a shake or two, and making off again. The horses, having ben tied up for an imergency, was easy gotten hold of so the men were close at the heels of the stock but could not get them back into the Correll. By the way one of the guards was ran over by the cattle and badly hurt. But we were ready for any imergency, having a Doctor along who soon patched him up again. So we were not detained long on account of our stampeed. When we started from our native town there happened to be an invaliad with us that was trying to elude the feld-istrayer death, She having consumption. She drove the horses into camp holding the lines in her own hands one evening, and about midnight the camp was aroused by the Scream of her mother that she was dead. True enough she was. So we prepared to render the last sad rights to the dead by taking of our boxes what we had made a rude Coffin and laid her to rest on the lonely plains of Platt River. It was not like laying our loved ones away in a nice Cemetery where we can go and strew their graves with flowers, but where you must take a last sad look of the fresh-made mound then move on. Well we were on the Platt river proper on the north bank fording deep streams almost daily. Our company elected a Captain before starting on this long journey, one that said he had already crossed the continent twice. When we came to the ferry on Platt River there was hundreds of wagons waiting to be ferried over which would cause a week of delay. So our captain throught best we should keep up on the north side of the River. All day long we had noticed the distant rumbling of thunder with an occasional shower. When we reaced the ford of Loop fork of the Platte we found it rising so the orders was to cross as many wagons that evening as possible. The men went to work with a will. They forded about one half of the wagons over that night then drove all the cattle over for the grass was better on the other side of the River. During the night there came up a terrific storm of rain & wind, blew all our tents down. The men had to run the wagons side by side as close as possible to keep them from turning over. While the storm raged the women & children were in the wagons expecting to be rolled over and over. But in the morning the storm was over but we had a rushing River before us. What next. We had kept some of the horses on our sid so as our captain thought best. The captain with some others rode over to a large timber Island in this streem, brought back a good report that by diving (driving) onto that Island we would have but a small stream to contend with but our oxen were on the other side. But here comes som more deluded emigrants and to the Island they went loaned us their cattle and on we went but Oh horrors the stream kept on rising until our little Island was laced by streams running in every way. Well after 9 days of suspence there was a rumor of lynching if something was not done. Well as we had plenty of Tar along it was proposed to take of the best wagon beds and cork and Tar them to prevent leaking. So at it they went and by the 11 night we were all safely over. Well right here i must say that i wached every load with a throbbing heart knowing my turn must soon come. Bye and by i took my three little children, took my seat with a norwegian man at the oars. When nearly half way out struck one of those trees that bob up and down, broke one oar. There was no other way then but let the thing drift back to the same side. Well we landed on the verry lower end of the Sand beach. But they soon had another oar and we were off again with no accident this time. Well we are all safe accross and each heart beats lighter. While on this Island we had such grand view of heards of Buffalo the verry earth shook by reason of their number. We again take up the line of march, days of ploughing through sun & sand, crossing deep streams. One day we heard a deep rumbling noise, our captain called a halt. In a few minute looking in the direction of the noise we saw the Buffalo coming. They always travail in a short gallop never turning for any thing. The heard passed in less than a quarter of a mile. The men thought to have a little fun, they would take their guns a shoot among them but seeing a better thing a calf had fallen behind the heard so they shot it down and that gave the women and children a chance to see how a Buffalo did look. Then they dressed it and all had plenty of Buffalo beef to do for days. I think it was the best meat i have ever tasted. Well for days it was verry monotinous, plenty of sand and hot winds. Once we ran a little risk of our lives, this was on what was marked deep crick. It was verry narrow but oh so deep, it being where the crick emtied in to Platt River. There was no bridge so the men cut down small cottonwood trees and made a bridge by laying the long ones for stringers and piling the brush crosswise. They would run the wagons down on this by hand and the teamster was ready with oxen and a long chain in hand ready to hook in the steaple in the end of the wagon tong to pull it over. Now this was my personal experiance. When the wagon was down on this frail bridge the teamster was fifty yards away at a little canvas tent drinking whisky. My husband seeing the situation ran that distance, got the cattle, but by this time the water was in the wagon bed. They hitched on but the wagon had settled until the brush all slipped before the wheels, but we got out safe. Now don't think i am all the one that had an experiance, but its my own i am writing.

There is many things could be said such as seeing the long black hair of women and the bones of people that had ben burried, then dug up by the kyotes and the flesh knawed clean from the bones. Well our last camp on Platte River is now reached and we all lay over and celebrate the 4 of July. We are leaving Fort Larima (Laramie) in the distance behind, travailing over rough sandy country, steering for sweet water, a small stream, at last we reach it, traval for days along its banks crossing & recrossing it. Nothing unusual, there is plenty of Deer, Antelope, Kiotes and Indians on the way now. No lack of good fresh meat. We pass the Independent rock (Independence Rock) on Sweet Water. At last we are at the Devels gate (Devil's Gate) on Sweet water. Here we leave one of our wagons. Here two families climb into one wagon and on we go. There is many things to be learned on a trip like this: every one will show his or her true character. We seem to partake of the wild nature of every thing. We are now in the great mormon country, Utah Territory.

Now this writing is renewed this the first day of our Lord 1905. There are many things that i shal omit having grown dim in my mind. We have never seen a house since crossing the Missouri River but now we come to where for the love of gain the Salt Lake people keep us well supplied with fresh sweet vegetables as we ever picked from our own gardens for which we were thankful. Their little cloth tents were dotted along the way for at least 200 miles.

Now we leave them no more fresh vegetables but sand & Indians. We come now to the Bear River country travail for weeks among the Siox tribe of indians. They were verry friendly. We now come to the 70 mile desert to Green River. Now we are coming into the rough country of the Rockies, travail over patches of Snow in midsummer, over hills and valeys for hundreds of miles. Have many stampeeds of the stock by Indians, one i will mention. Our stock took fright at night, started with all Speed for the mountains, the night watch keeping in hearing of the bells for miles, all at once the bells ceased and waited until morning. When day dawned they were on the side of a mountain that overlooked a beautiful little valey, there the stock all stood with not a soul in sight. After the boys got the cattle started back over the road they had just pased over in the dark, they almost shuddered to think what a misstep would have done for them. Only an Indian trail far up on the side of a shetrock mountain. They got back with all the stock, now for a half days drive. Tonight they go again, this time they jump them off a bank 10 or 15 feet high into a small stream and hold them there until late in the day. The men got onto their track found where they had rushed them over the bank, there they were in the water and the Indians lying in the grass keeping them in there. The boys said some of the reds jumped six feet in the air never to drive another lot of emigrats cattle off. Another half days drive.

Now I must tel you what brought all this about. You know that the Indians are great beggars if you know any thing of their trait of character. Our captain became exasperated at them so when he saw some coming he let his large bulldog loose from his chain and one bound and he had torn a piece of skin from the Indians thigh as large as ones hand. They left muttering revenge so we all had to bear the blame of the Indian blood and suffer alike.

Aug. 13th 1905

I will try again to renew my narritive of the Plains. We are leaving many hundred[s] of miles behind us. We are nearing the Humbolt country with not much variation. Plenty of Sagebrush & Sand. After miles of travail we leave Humbolt, part of the train keeping down the River, the rest of us coming to Oregon. Here comes a sad farewell, many of us had started together from our native home, here to say the sadest of words—farewell.

Now each take their way, some for California, some for Oregon.

Water is verry scarce now. At last we are nearing the Sirena evada mountains. At the foot of the mountain we camped on Tula Lake, plenty of
water and good grass. This night our Cattle was turned on the Lake to
range with but few herders. The Indians seeing their opportunity lost no
time. The Stock was ran of up into a cove of the mountain and 13 head
of our best oxen killed and cut up nicely. In the morning our men took
horses and carried to camp as much of the best of the meat as they
thought could possibly be used so we had plenty of beef for many days,
but I pity the Indian that eat a bite of the meat that was left.

Now how were we to move, cant with 13 of our Cattle gone. Well we
all divided up our teems until we moved out. This brought us to the crossing of the Sirena Mt. It took all day to get over. The men would take as
many wagons as they could find teems for up the summit, then come
down and get dinner, hitch on to the remainder and go to the top. It was
a lovely spot on the top of this mountain. You could see the Goose Lake
at its foot seemingly but a mile away, but we came down the mountain and
made our camp at its foot. The next day we travailed over juniper ridges
all day. At night came to the beautiful waters of Goose Lake. Here is a
Babe Born to be laid away on the outlet of this beautiful Lake. But no
time to lay bye for sickness so we travailed on for days when our hearts
were made glad one day to see a company of white coming to meet us.
They proved to be a relief company sent out by California & Oregon with
provision for any that might be destitute. Here was a Dr. with his services
for the sick who kept this poor Lady and her family until the volenteers
came in that fall, but only to get her into civilation to bury her. We are
now travailing over the high range of the Siscue mountains. While eating
breakfast one morning a huge black Bear trotted by our camp and seemed
surprised to see people away out there. We are now out of sight of
Klameth Lake in the heart of the mountain but right here we had rogues.

My Husband had a large mare worth $300 if he had got in to the valey with her. Another man in the company had a fine match for her in size & color. It was this mans duty to drive the loose stock and at camping time both of these mares were missing. So in the morning men stopped back to look for the last horses, but this was the last we ever seen of them. But a year after a friend of ours saw this verry same man in Yreka, California with both of the mares and ours had a fine colt by her side.

Now we are almost through the Siscue mountains, coming on top of a high ridge we saw what gladdened all our heart. The woman threw their bonnets up in the air for we were in sight of Civilation once more. That night we camped near a house. This place belonged to a man that had came with most of us from the Misouri river. His wife invited some of us to take a walk with her to see garden, it did our eyes good to see a garden growing once more. And when i saw the squashes i told her i would have my husband come in the morning before we left to get one. After he got it asked the price, $1.00, so after that for many years we raised the dollar Squash in Rogue River valey. Well we moved on down Bear creck near jacksonville. Here we camped while the men went out to look for land. In a few days they all dame back well pleased and we seperated, each family to take possession of their donation claim. With our family of 3 children we took up our claim 15 miles North of jacksonville. This was in the fall of Fifty 3. And now we must begin life anew. We got a little log house up to live in and the wild grass & clover was good, so we had plenty of milk & Butter. My Husband bought a new Plough and comenced to open a new farm. Now our first seed wheat cost us 5 dollars per bushel so two bushels was all we could get. So in the spring of 54 we sowed that.

During this summer we ploughed ground enough to sow the entire crop from the two bushels. Now our thrasting machine was a rail pen four rails high covered with rails. ON this we laid the wheat, a few bundles at a time, then a long stick and beat it out. When done threshing we took a canvass, put into that a small amount of wheat at a time. Taking this by the four corners we cleaned out the chaff by the wind seperating the wheat from the chaff. In the spring of 55 we sowed our crop and harvested it, threshed it out with horses this time, got a fanning Mill, cleaned it al up, put it in the bin. We thought we were going finely but Oh horrors we had only ben working for the Indians all this time. For on Oct the 10 1855 the first battle was fought between the whites and indians which has already gone into history. And now my husband being dead i am living off the Pension granted by the goverment for labour done by the Volunteers of Oregon. The end.

RULES OF THE ROAD

John McDannald

> *It is easy for a modern reader to imagine travel along the Oregon Trail as a mostly tidy western motion in single file along a well-worn track, but that was hardly the case. The Oregon Trail was a network of trails, side trails, and short-cuts. The many thousands of wagons that moved west in the direction of California and Oregon didn't follow signposts or written regulations. There were common rules of courtesy, however, that emigrants hoped their fellow wayfarers would follow.*

As we are now following as closely as possible along the banks of Cache Lapondria in order to cross over this range of mountains out into the Laramie Plains, by way of the pass at its headwaters and Virginia Dale, we encounter some extremely rough and narrow road. There were certain unwritten but well recognized rules of etiquette of today. And the infraction of this unwritten law or acknowledged customs and practices of that time was not only looked upon with disfavor, but any man who repeated the offense seldom escaped with anything less than a severe reprimand, and a warning that it must not be repeated. It had always been mutually agreed that one team would not pass another while both were moving along the same road, unless the team in the lead had stopped to rest or to make alterations or repairs to either the harness or wagon; then it was permissible for the rear team to pass around the other wagon and take the lead.

THE EQUIPMENT, SUPPLIES, AND THE METHOD OF TRAVELING

Lansford W. Hastings' The Emigrants' Guide to Oregon and California

> *Lansford Hastings had this practical advice to offer would-be emigrants in his famous guidebook.*

In treating of the equipment, supplies, and the method of traveling, I shall confine my remarks, entirely, to the over land route, which lies through the great southern pass; as the chief emigration, to those countries, is, at this time, by that route, which from present indications, is destined to become the great thoroughfare, between the States, and both Oregon and California. All persons, designing to travel by this route, should, invariably, equip themselves with a good gun; at least, five pounds of powder, and twenty pounds of lead; in addition to which, it might be advisable, also, for each to provide himself with a holster of good pistols, which would, always, be found of very great service, yet they are not indispensable. If pistols are taken, an additional supply of ammunition should, also, be taken; for, it almost necessarily follows, that the more firearms you have, the more ammunition you will require, whether assailed by the Indians, or assailing the buffalo. If you come in contact with the latter, you will find the pistols of the greatest importance; for you may gollop your horse, side by side, with them, and having pistols, you may shoot them down at your pleasure; but should you come in mortal conflict with the former, the rifle will be found to be much more effective, and terrific; the very presence of which, always, affords ample security. Being provided with arms and ammunition, as above suggested, the emigrant may consider himself, as far as his equipment is concerned, prepared, for any warlike emergency, especially, if nature has, also, equipped him with the requisite energy and courage.

In procuring supplies for this journey, the emigrant should provide himself with, at least, two hundred pounds of flour, or meal; one hundred and fifty pounds of bacon; ten pounds of coffee; twenty pounds of sugar; and ten pounds of salt, with such other provisions as he may prefer, and can conveniently take; yet the provisions, above enumerated, are considered, ample, both as to quantity, and variety. It would, perhaps, be advisable for emigrants, not to encumber themselves with any other, than those just enumerated; as it is impracticable for them, to take all the luxuries, to which they have been accustomed; and as it is found, by experience, that, when upon this kind of expedition, they are not desired, even by the most devoted epicurean [sic]. The above remarks, in reference to the quantity of provisions, are designed to apply only to adults; but taking the above as the data, parents will find no difficulty, in determining as to the necessary quantum for children; in doing which, however, it should always be observed, that children as well as adults, require, about twice the quantity of provisions, which they would, at home, for the same length of time. This is attributable to their being deprived of vegetables, and other sauce, and their being confined to meat and bread alone; as well as the fact, of their being subjected to continued and regular exercise, in the open air, which gives additional vigor and strength, which, greatly improves the health, and therefore, gives an additional demand for food. I am aware, that an opinion prevails among many, that when arriving in that region in which the buffalo abound, meat can be very readily obtained, and hence, much less meat need be taken; but this is in error, which, unless cautiously guarded against, will be very, apt to prove fatal: for to be found in that wild and remote region, depending upon the buffalo for meat, would, in nine cases out of ten, result in immediate or ultimate starvation, especially, if there should be large body of persons together. It is true, that immense herds of buffalo, are found in that region; but it would be impossible, to kill them in sufficient numbers, to sustain a large party, unless many, persons should devote their entire attention to the business of hunting; and, even then, it could not be done, unless the company should delay for that purpose, which would, in all probability, produce consequences, equally as fatal as starvation; for, unless you pass over the mountains early in the fall, you are very liable to be detained, by impassable mountains of snow, until the next spring, or, perhaps, forever. Then it would seem, that, although the buffalo are vastly numerous, they cannot be relied upon; yet to avoid encumbering himself with the very large quantities of meat which his family would require, the emigrant can drive cattle, which will afford him a very good substitute, not only for the beef of the buffalo, but, also, for bacon; and what is more important, is, that they can be relied upon, under all circumstances.

Very few cooking utensils, should be taken, as they very, much increase the load, to avoid which, is always a consideration of paramount importance. A baking-kettle, frying-pan, tea-kettle, tea-pot, and coffee-pot, are all the furniture of this kind, that is essential, which, together with tin plates, tin cups, ordinary knives, forks, spoons, and.a coffee-mill, should constitute the entire kitchen apparatus. Bedding should consist of nothing more than blankets, sheets, coverlets and pillows, which, being spread upon a buffalo robe, an oiled cloth, or some other impervious substance, should constitute the beds, which are found much preferable, because of their being much less bulky, and weighty. Feather-beds are sometimes taken by the families, but in many instances, they find them, not only burthensome and inconvenient, but entirely useless, consequently, they leave them by the way, and pursue the course above suggested. Our common horses are preferable for the saddle, but it becomes necessary to take such numbers of them, that they may be occasionally changed; for it is found by experience, that no American horse can be taken entirely through, being daily used, either under the saddle, or in the harness. Many prefer mules for the saddle, but they are objectionable, because of their extreme intractability, and their inflexible inertness, in which they appear to indulge, to a much greater extent than usual, upon this kind of expedition. For the harness, mules are preferable to horses; for, notwithstanding their extreme inertness and slowness, they are found to endure the fatigue and to subsist upon vegetation alone, much better than horses; but oxen are considered preferable to either. If mules are taken, it is advisable to take more of them, than are required for ordinary teams, in order that they maybe changed as occasion may require; for they, even, frequently become so fatigued, and exhausted, that they, like the horses, are left by the way, to be taken or killed, by the Indians. Oxen endure the fatigue and heat, much better than either horses or mules; and they also, subsist much better, upon vegetation alone, as all herds are, of course, required to do, upon all portions of the route. There is no instance, within my knowledge, of any emigrants being required to leave his oxen by the way, because of excessive fatigue, or extreme poverty; for, as a general thing, they continue to thrive, during the entire journey. But there are other considerations, which give them a decided preference, among which is the fact, that they are not liable to be stolen by the Indians, who are aware, that they travel so extremely slowly, that it would be impossible for them, to drive them so far, during the night, that they could not be retaken, during the next day; hence, they will not hazard the attempt, especially as they would be serviceable to them, only as food; and as the country abounds with buffalo, and other game, the meat of which they very much prefer. Another consideration, which gives cattle the preference, is that they do not ramble far from the encampment, as do horses and mules; nor are they necessarily tied, or otherwise confined, but are permitted to range about uncontrolled, both by day and night; and, yet they are always to be found, within sight or hearing of the encampment. In selecting horses, mules and oxen, for this expedition, none should be taken, which are under five, or over ten years of age; nor should calves or colts, under one year of age, be taken; for, from the tenderness of their hoofs, and their inability otherwise to endure fatigue, they are invariably left by the way. The hoofs of older cattle, even, are frequently worn to such an extent, that, at times, it appears almost impossible, for them to continue the journey, but being driven on, from day to day, their hoofs soon become again so indurated, as to obviate all further inconvenience. Some urge the propriety of working cows, instead of oxen, both the advantage and propriety of which, are very questionable; for, it will be admitted, that they are much inferior to oxen, in point of physical strength, and, hence, cannot be as serviceable for the draught; but it is urged, that, although they are more feeble, and, hence, less serviceable for the yoke, yet they are preferable, because they answer the double purpose draught animals, and milk-cows; but the force of this reason is lost, when we take into consideration, the unwholesomeness of the milk of animals, whose systems are, thus, enfevered by exposure to excessive heat, and extreme physical exertion.

Good and substantial wagons should always be selected, and however firm and staunch they may appear, they should, invariably, be particularly examined, and repaired, before leaving the States; for, otherwise, the emigrant may set out, with a very good wagon to all appearances, the defects of which, when he shall have traveled a few hundred miles, will have become very obvious; the consequence of which, is, that he is left without a wagon, and thrown upon the kindness of his friends, for the conveyance of his family and provisions. Whether wagons are new or old, it is perhaps, preferable, always to have the tires re-set, previous to leaving Independence; otherwise, before traveling one thousand miles, into that vastly elevated region, from the intense heat of those extensive, sandy plains, and the extreme aridity of the atmosphere, the tires become so expanded, and the wooden portions of the wheels, so contracted, that it will be very difficult to keep them together, in which, however, by the constant and regular application of water, you may possibly succeed. Those who go to Oregon, if they design to perform the journey in the ordinary time, of 120 days, should take their wagons, with a view of leaving them at Fort Hall, and performing the residue of the journey, on horseback; otherwise, the repeated interruptions, below that point, will, most likely, present an insuperable barrier, to the accomplishment of their object. Horses, which have been accustomed to wearing shoes, should also be shod for this journey, but others should not, as to shoe the latter, only imposes an unnecessary expense, and spoils the hoof, by cutting away that horny substance, which, hardened by the intensely heated sand, would answer all the purposes of shoes. Mules, like horses, if they have not been previously shod, ought not to be, for the same reason, as that above stated; and oxen and cows, ought never to be shod; yet many pursue a different course, and thereby, incur much useless expense, and inconvenience. Those horses and mules, which it becomes necessary to shoe, should be shod, previous to leaving the States; and one or two pairs of extra shoes, should be taken for each, which may be set by the blacksmiths on the way; as there are, always, several mechanics of that kind, belonging to each company. Besides the foregoing supplies, emigrants should also, provide themselves with good wagon covers and tents, tent poles, axes, spades, and hoes, as well as strong ropes, of about sixty feet in length, for each horse or mule, with a supply of stakes, to which they are to be tied; in addition to which, every wagon should be supplied with extra axletrees, chains, hammers, and the like; and the different mechanics should also take a small portion of their tools, as they are, always, needed by the way. Should there be physicians and surgeons, attached to the company, as there most usually are, they should supply themselves with a small assortment of medicine, and a few surgical instruments. In addition to all the foregoing, perhaps, it would also be advisable for each emigrant, to provide himself with some such goods, as are adapted to the Indian trade, such, for instance, as beads, tobacco, handkerchiefs, blankets, ready made clothing, such as cheap, summer coats, pantaloons, vests and course, cheap shirts, butcher knives, fishhooks, and powder and lead. Being equipped and supplied, as here suggested, the emigrant may set out upon this wild, yet interesting excursion, with high prospects of enjoying many extraordinary and pleasing scenes; and of safely arriving at his desired place of destination, without suffering any of that extraordinary toil, unheard of hardship, or eminent danger, which his own fruitful imagination, or the kind regard of his numerous friends, may have devised.

Nothing now remains to be done, but to notice the method of traveling, which I shall proceed to do, with as much brevity, as is consistent with the importance of the subject. Emigrants should, invariably, arrive at Independence, Mo., on, or before, the fifteenth day of April, so as to be in readiness, to enter upon their journey, on or before, the first day of May; after which time, they should never start if it can, possibly, be avoided. The advantages to be derived, from setting out at as early a day as that above suggested, are those of having an abundance of good pasturage, in passing over those desolate and thirsty plains; and being enabled to cross the mountains, before the falling of mountains of snow, or floods of rain, which usually occurs, in that region, early in October. Before leaving the rendezvous, emigrants should, always, organize, by dividing into such companies, and electing such officers, as shall be deemed necessary. Having organized, they commence their onward, westward march, under the direction of their officers, and moving merrily on, they soon arrive at their mid-day encampment, when the wagons are driven up, so as to form a large elliptical enclosure, into which the horses may be driven, in case of an incursion, or an attack by the Indians. This enclosure is called a "caral," and is formed, by dividing the whole number of wagons, into equal divisions, each of which, is under the control of an officer, who is designated for that purpose, and who moves on, in advance of his particular division, to the place pointed out, by the principal officer, as the encampment where one of the wagons of each division, is placed at the head of the encampment, side by side, about ten feet distant from each other. By the side of each of these, and about half the length of the wagon, to the rear of each, is another wagon driven; at the side, and half to the rear, of the latter wagons, are two others driven, and so on continually, until the rear of the enclosure, is as nearly, closed as the front. The cattle and horses, are now turned loose, upon the plains, where they are guarded and herded, by a guard, consisting of several persons, who are designated for that purpose; and who remain upon the plains, beyond the herds, until all have dined, and until the command is given to prepare to march, when they, immediately commence to drive the herds from all directions, toward the camp. Each now proceeds to catch, harness and saddle his horses, and yoke his oxen; and soon the caravan is again in motion; and moving onward, with increased speed, it arrives, in a few hours, at the nocturnal encampment. At this encampment, as at the former, the wagons are again divided, into two equal divisions, which now move, side by side, following their respective officers, until they arrive at the place designated, as the encampment. Here one of the officers, followed by his division, falls off to the right, and the other, to the left, forming right angles; and moving in opposite directions, to designated points, when the former division wheels to the left, and the latter, to the right, forming right angles, as before; when moving on, to another designated point, the former division again wheels to the left and the latter, to the right forming right angles, and continuing the same direction, until the two divisions, meet, and thus form large square "caral" or enclosure. Horses are now unharnessed; cattle are unyoked and all are turned together, upon the unbounded plains, where they are permitted to graze, under the watchful care of a vigilant guard, until nightfall; when after all have supped, and the cloths are removed, the command is given, and the vast herds are crowded together, into the enclosure, before described; which is, now, everywhere surrounded, with erected tents and blazing fires. Within this "caral" or enclosure, stakes are thickly driven, to which the horses and mules, are firmly tied; when sufficient guards are sent out and stationed, at designated posts, where they remain for about two hours; when they are relieved by others, who, after the lapse of two hours, are also relieved, in a similar manner, and so on, during the night. In the morning, upon the signal's being given, other guards are sent into the plains, in the vicinity of the camp, in order to receive and guard the horses and mules, as they are turned out of the "caral," and until the command is given to march, when the tumultuous caravan is again in motion, amid the deafening confusion of the loquacious, noisy thousands.

Nothing different from the foregoing, worthy of remark, occurs, from day to day, in reference to the method of traveling, until the company arrives in the territory of the hostile Indians, which commences at the Kansas river, and extends throughout the residue of the journey. Throughout all portions of the country, beyond the Kansas, emigrants are required to proceed with much more caution, especially, in the country of the Pawnees, Sioux, Shyanes, Eutaws, and Black-feet. Wherever there are evidences of hostile Indians' being in the vicinity of the company, it is advisable, always, to enjoin upon all, to avoid a separation from the main body of the company, and, at the same time, to keep an advance and rear-guard out, as the company is on the march. Should the guards discover an approaching enemy, the safest course is, to throw the caravan, at once, into a defensive attitude, which is very readily done, by forming a "caral," in a manner, quite similar to that first described; the only difference being, that the teams of both cattle and horses, occupy the interior, instead of the exterior, of the "caral," without being detached from the wagons. Being thus formed, the entire caravan assumes an impregnable attitude; the wagons affording complete protection to the women and children, as well as the teams, and at the same time, affording a secure breast-work for the men, should they be driven to the necessity of using them for that purpose. Upon the approach of the Indians, and their friendly designs, timidity or cowardice being discovered, the company is soon enabled to continue its march, as though no interruption had occurred. Upon many portions of the route, it becomes necessary thus to form the wagons, several times each day, in order to dispose of various marauding and war parties, with whom emigrants, frequently come in contact. In many portions of this country, it is found to be unsafe, to turn the horses or mules loose, upon the plains, either at night or during the day; instead of which course, they should be tied with long ropes to stakes, which are driven for that purpose, being well guarded, and moved from time to time, as circumstances may require. Whether this course should be pursued, is, of course, determined by the officers, in view of all the surrounding circumstances, which if adopted, is found to answer every purpose, of turning the horses and mules loose upon the plains; and it is much more convenient, as they are much more readily taken, when the company is in readiness to march. A sufficient and vigilant guard, should, always, be kept out, whenever the company is encamped, whether during the day or night. These guards maybe distinguished, as day, and night guards, the former of which, should always be sent out, whether in the morning or at noon, before the horses and mules are turned out, in order to receive them, and the more effectually, to prevent their rambling far from the encampment, as well as the more readily to drive them in to the "caral," in case of an incursion by the Indians. The night guard should, always, be sent out previous to nightfall; when the fires should, invariably, be extinguished, in order to prevent being discovered by the Indians, from the surrounding hills and mountains. The day guards should not generally, be permitted to discharge a gun, only in case of an attack, as the discharge of firearms by the guard, is considered, as an indication of the hostile movements of the enemy; nor are the night guards ever permitted to discharge their firearms, unless human beings are descried, endeavoring to effect either a clandestine, or forcible approach.

The Indians, being aware of this arrangement among mountaineers, have, in many instances availed themselves of the preference, which the above arrangements, give animals, in quadruped form, to those in human form. Being aware that, in human form, it would be very dangerous to approach the encampment of white men, in the night, they change their forms, and approach in the form of an elk, or some other familiar animal; but they usually prefer the form of the elk, as it is the most common animal in those regions. In order to effect the requisite metamorphosis, to enable them to enter the camp of the whites, they prepare the hide of an elk, entire, retaining his ponderous horns, which being thus prepared, is placed upon one of the most daring "braves," who proceeds to the encampment; and, upon all fours, moves about the camp, apparently feeding as he goes, until he observes the greatest space between the sentinels, when he passes on, elk like, among the horses. He now goes on, from horse to horse, cutting the ropes with which they are tied, until he has loosed a greater part of them, when he throws off his disguise, mounts a horse, and, with most hideous whoops and yells, unlike an elk; he soon puts the horses to flight, and the guard to a nonplus; and leaving all in the utmost confusion, gallops swiftly away closely pursuing his numerous, frightened prey, when, soon, he is joined by hundreds of his villainous comrades. With the precaution, however, of securing the horses properly, within the "caral," as before suggested, no danger whatever is; to be apprehended from the elk, in human form. Another method, by which the Indians effect an entrance into the encampment by deceptive means is by drawing near to the camp, in various directions and commencing a most tremendous howling, in precise imitation of wolves; and so perfect is the mimicry, that it is almost impossible to distinguish their howl, from that of the real wolf. By this deceptive course, the sentinels are thrown off their guard; for as they hear what they suppose to be wolves, in almost every direction from the encampment, and that too, very near, they are naturally led to the conclusion, that there are no Indians their vicinity, as wolves and Indians seldom occupy the same country together in harmony. In order to avoid the misfortunes which so frequently befall emigrants from the accidental discharge of firearms, guns should never be carried capped or primed; yet they should, always, be carried loaded, and otherwise in order for action, upon a moment's warning. More danger is to be apprehended, from your own guns, without the observance of the above precaution, than from those of the enemy; for we very frequently, hear of emigrants' being killed from the accidental discharge of firearms; but we very seldom hear of their being killed by Indians. The importance of observing the above regulation, cannot be too strongly urged; for as the entire company, of hundreds or thousands as the case may be, is frequently thrown together, and confined within a very small compass, the accidental discharge of a gun, is likely to be attended with serious and fatal consequences. A practice prevails among the emigrants, of disbanding, and disposing of their arms to the Indians and others, upon arriving at Green river, or Fort Hall, and pursuing the residue of the journey, in detached and unarmed companies. This practice should, by all means, be invariably avoided, as it is beyond those points that the Black-feet, the most hostile tribe in all that region, are met, if they are at all seen; and as all the Indians, who inhabit that portion of the country, although they are said to be friendly, as before remarked, avail themselves of every opportunity, of insulting, and even robbing, every small party, with whom, they may chance to meet. Both numbers and arms, sufficient for self-protection, are as indispensably necessary, upon this, as upon any other portion of the route; although an adverse opinion, is prevalent, among all the mountaineers, of that region, yet experience, amply sustains the opinion, just advanced.

In hunting the buffalo, the greatest precaution should be observed, as the hunters are not, unfrequently, attacked and robbed, of both their meat and horses; hence, it is advisable, that they should, always go out, in sufficient numbers, to insure their protection. The method of taking the buffalo, is either by approaching them unobserved, or by giving them chase, on horseback, and shooting them down as you pass them: the latter of which methods is, perhaps, preferable; and, hence, it is most generally adopted. In hunting the buffalo, emigrants are very liable to loose their fleet horses, which, after having been used a few times in the chase, with whatever timidity, they may have, at first, approached the buffalo, will, the moment buffalo are seen, evince the greatest anxiety to commence the chase; and, if restrained, in the least, they prance to and fro, under the steady restraint of the rider, or standing, they gnash the bit, and stamp and paw the ground, with all the wild ferocity, of those trained for the race course, or the battle field; and, unless perfectly secured, by being permanently tied or held, they dart away, and commence the chase without a rider. There have been numerous instances, upon the appearance of the buffalo, of their having broken loose in this manner, although saddled and permanently tied; and having commenced the chase at the top of their speed, until they arrived in the midst of the buffalo, when horses and buffalo together, leaped away over the vast plains, and were never seen or heard of afterwards. Companies should never consist of more than five hundred persons; for, as they are enlarged, the inconvenience, difficulties and dangers, are increased. The inconvenience of encamping a large company upon the very small encampments, to which emigrants are frequently necessarily confined, the difficulty of obtaining a sufficiency of pasturage, for such extensive herds; and the increased danger, arising from accidents, where large bodies of armed men, are thrown together, without the aid of military discipline; as well as the inconvenience and difficulty, arising from the protracted marches of large caravans, and the danger arising from the extreme tardiness, with which large companies, are thrown into a defensive attitude, in case of an attack, must be obvious to all, even the most inexperienced, in this method of traveling. By the careful observance, of the foregoing directions and suggestions, as well as a close adherence to their own experience, emigrants will avoid all those hardships and dangers, which they would; otherwise necessarily experience. It is true, that emigrants in traveling, through these wild regions are cut off in a measure, from society, deprived of many of the luxuries of civilized life; and it is also true, that their way is not studded, with magnificent churches, and spacious houses of public entertainment; but they have enough of the enjoyments of society, for their present purposes, and as many of the luxuries of life, as are conducive to health and happiness: and although they have not the benefits of churches, yet every camp of the emigrants is truly, a camp-meeting, and presents many of the exciting and interesting scenes, exhibited upon those important occasions; and, although they have not all the conveniences, of commodious public-houses, yet nature's great inn, is always in readiness for their reception; and they experience the continual manifestations of the peculiar care and protection, of its great Proprietor, whether high upon the eternal mountains above, or deep, in the untrodden vales below.

The task assigned me at the outset, I have now, faithfully, though briefly, and imperfectly, performed; yet, notwithstanding its brevity and imperfection, it is hoped that it will afford some valuable and practical information, in reference to both those highly important countries. Nothing, however, has been attempted, but an extremely brief, though practical description of those countries, which was designed, to enable the reader, to draw tolerably correct conclusions, in reference to their extent, mountains, rivers, lakes, islands, harbors, soil, climate, health, productions, governments, society, trade and commerce; and to give the emigrant, such practical information, relative to the routes, the equipment, supplies, and the method of traveling, as is thought to be essential, to his success and safety: all of which, I have now done, as far as consisent with the extent of this little work, and my original design. In leaving this subject it is natural for us, not only to review what we have just seen, in reference to those countries, and to contemplate their present, prosperous condition, but also, to anticipate their condition, in reference to the progressive future. In view of their increasing population, accumulating wealth, and growing prosperity, I can not but believe, that the time is not distant, when those wild forests, trackless plains, untrodden valleys, and the unbounded ocean, will present one grand scene, of continuous improvements, and unparalleled commerce: when those vast forests, shall have disappeared, before the hardy pioneer; those extensive plains, shall abound with innumerable herds, of domestic animals; those fertile valleys, shall groan under the immense weight of their abundant products: when those numerous rivers, shall team with countless steamboats, steamships, ships, barques and brigs; when the entire country, be everywhere intersected, with turnpike roads, railroads and canals; and when, all the vastly numerous, and rich resources, of that now, almost unknown region, will be fully and advantageously developed. To complete this picture, we may fancy to ourselves, a Boston, a New York, a Philadelphia and a Baltimore growing up in a day, as it were, both in Oregon and California, crowded with a vast population, and affording all the enjoyments and luxuries, of civilized life. And to this we may add, numerous churches, magnificent edifices, spacious colleges, and stupendous monuments and observatories, all of Grecian architecture, rearing their majestic heads, high in the aerial region, amid those towering pyramids of perpetual snow, looking down upon all the busy, bustling scenes, of tumultuous civilization, amid the eternal verdure of perennial spring. And in fine, we are also led to contemplate the time, as fast approaching, when the supreme darkness of ignorance, superstition, and despotism, which now, so entirely pervade many portions of those remote regions, will have fled forever, before the march of civilization, and the blazing light, of civil and religious liberty; when genuine republicanism, and unsophisticated democracy, shall be reared up, and tower aloft, even upon the now wild shores, of the great Pacific; where they shall forever stand forth, as enduring monuments, to the increasing wisdom of man, and the infinite kindness and protection, of an all-wise, and overruling Providence.

SOURCES

Arthur, David. "Across the Plains in 1843: Arthur's Prairie First Furrow Plowed in Clackamas County." *Sunday Oregonian,* 1889.

Breen, Patrick. *The Diary of Patrick Breen: One of the Donner Party.* Edited by Frederick J. Teggart. Berkeley: The University Press, 1910.

Burnett, Lucy Jane Hall. "Reminiscences of a Trip Across the Plains in '45." In *Souvenir of Western Women,* by Mary Osborn Douthit. Portland, Ore.: Anderson and Dunway Company, 1905

Campbell, David. "Sketch of the hardships endured by those who crossed the plains in '46." *Weekly Review,* Porterville, Calif., July 1899.

Finley, Newton G. *Memoirs of Travel, 1852.* (Written December 30, 1922.) Family History Library, Salt Lake City, microfilm #1206424, item 17.

Hastings, Lansford W. *The Emigrants' Guide to Oregon and California.* Cincinnati: George Conclin Publisher, 1845.

Holliday, J. S. *The World Rushed In: The California Gold Rush Experience.* New York: Simon and Schuster, 1981.

Holmes, Kenneth, ed. *Covered Wagon Women.* Vol. 4. Glendale: The Arthur H. Clark Company, 1988.

Longmire, James. "Interesting Story of His Experience in Hunting Buffalo Coming Across the Plains." *Tacoma Sunday Ledger*, 21 August 1892.

McClain, Martha Ann Tuttle. Reminiscences of Martha Ann Tuttle McClain: From Iowa to Oregon, via the Applegate Trail. Transcribed from the Oregon Historical Society's manuscript collections, 1903–1905.

Sager, Catherine. *Across the Plains in 1844.* Glen Adams Publishing, 1989.

Thurman, Sue Bailey. *Pioneers of Negro Origin in California.* San Francisco: Acme Pub. Co., 1952.

Whitman, Narcissa P. *The Letters of Narcissa Whitman.* Fairfield, Wash.: Ye Galleon Press, 1986